ood that better coordination of these ac-
vities will be a prerequisite for increased
nding. They identify the obstacles to
eating a more effective and efficient sys-
m, and they weigh the prospects for build-
g a unified, cooperative adult education
terprise.

The result is an integrated overview of
ult education today and of its prospects
the future. Instructors and specialists
ll improve their understanding of this
t-evolving field, and program planners
d administrators will derive a clearer
w of how their specific objectives can be
thered by greater coordination of the
ult education movement.

THE AUTHORS

ᴴᴺ M. Peters is professor of continuing
d higher education at the University of
nnessee.

The other authors are identified in the
nt of the book.

A publication in
The Adult Education Association
Handbook Series in Adult Education

Building
an Effective
Adult Education
Enterprise

*John M. Peters
and Associates*

Building an Effective Adult Education Enterprise

Jossey-Bass Publishers
San Francisco • Washington • London • 1980

BUILDING AN EFFECTIVE ADULT EDUCATION ENTERPRISE
by John M. Peters and Associates

Copyright © 1980 by: Adult Education Association
of the United States of America
810 Eighteenth Street, N.W.
Washington, D.C. 20006

Jossey-Bass Inc., Publishers
433 California Street
San Francisco, California 94104

Jossey-Bass Limited
28 Banner Street
London EC1Y 8QE

Library of Congress Cataloging in Publication Data

Peters, John Marshall, 1941–
    Building an effective adult education enterprise.

    (Adult Education Association handbook series in adult education)
    Bibliography: p. 164
    Includes index.
    1. Adult education. I. Title. II. Series:
Adult Education Association. Adult Education Associa-
tion handbook series in adult education.
LC5215.P44   374   78-62573
ISBN 0-87589-455-0

Manufactured in the United States of America

JACKET DESIGN BY WILLI BAUM

FIRST EDITION

Code 8021

The AEA Handbook Series
in Adult Education

WILLIAM S. GRIFFITH
University of British Columbia
HOWARD Y. McCLUSKY
University of Michigan
General Editors

Edgar J. Boone
Ronald W. Shearon
Estelle E. White
and Associates
Serving Personal and
Community Needs Through
Adult Education
April 1980

John M. Peters
and Associates
Building an Effective
Adult Education
Enterprise
April 1980

Huey B. Long
Roger Hiemstra
and Associates
Changing Approaches
to Studying Adult
Education
April 1980

Foreword

Adult education as a field of study and of practice is not well understood by many literate and intelligent American adults whose exposure to the field has been limited to one or a few aspects of its apparently bewildering mosaic. Since 1926, when the American Association for Adult Education (AAAE) was founded, the leaders of that organization and its successor, the Adult Education Association of the U.S.A. (AEA), have striven to communicate both to the neophytes in the field and to the adult public an understanding of its diverse and complex enterprises. A major vehicle for accomplishing this communication has been a sequence of handbooks of adult education, issued periodically to convey a broad view of the mosaic. In 1934, 1936, and 1948 the AAAE published the first three handbooks. Although the Association had intended to issue a handbook every two years, that plan was not carried out for a number of reasons, including the outbreak of World War II and the termination of support by the Carnegie Corporation. Within three years of the publication of the 1948 handbook the Association itself dissolved in order to establish the AEA, which included the former members of both the AAAE and the Department of Adult Education of the National Education Association. It was nine years before the AEA was able to publish its first handbook, the fourth in the sequence, followed a decade later by the fifth version.

    In the early 1970s both the Publications Committee of AEA and the Commission of the Professors of Adult Education (an affiliated organization of the AEA) explored the kinds of handbooks that could be designed to serve the changing nature and needs of the field. They found that different parts of the field were developing at different rates—in some areas information was becoming outdated rapidly, whereas in others a decennial handbook would be adequate to maintain currency. Moreover, the growing literature and the many developments in policies and programs led them to conclude that a single volume of traditional size would not be sufficient to treat the expanding knowledge base, the changing policies and practices, and the controversial topics in adult education. Accordingly, the Publications Committee decided that the next handbook would consist of several volumes, allowing the presentation of an increased amount of information on each of nine selected parts of the field and preparing the way for subsequent revisions of each volume independently on a schedule reflecting the pace of change in each area. The result is The AEA Handbook Series on Adult Education, which is being developed by the general editors with the guidance and assistance of the Publications Committee.

Building an Effective Adult Education Enterprise was designed to provide an overview of the entire field, reflecting the multiple facets and their relationships. The other eight volumes deal with changing approaches to the study of adult education, serving community needs, administering adult education, redefining the discipline, responsibilities of adult education, comparative adult education, training, and instruction.

Preparation of the series required the cooperation and dedicated efforts of scores of chapter authors, Publication Committee chairmen and members, and successive executive committees of the AEA. In bringing together the insights and perceptions of adult education scholars, the series is a major contribution of the Association to the advancement of an understanding of adult education as a field of study and of practice.

January 1980   WILLIAM S. GRIFFITH
                                             HOWARD Y. MCCLUSKY
                                             General Editors

Preface

The plethora of definitions of adult education testify to the complexity of the field. Few tasks are as challenging to the adult educator as the problem of finding order within the collage of organizations, programs, clientele, and concepts that depicts the nature of adult education. But order must be found, definitions must be sharpened, and clarity must be gained if advances are to be made in the disciplined inquiry into adult education. This volume was compiled to study the nature of adult education from the perspective of how it is organized to fulfill its functions in society. Our goal is to increase understanding of the structure and function of adult education and to offer a prelude to further inquiry.

Work began on this volume of the Handbook Series with the assumption that an important contribution to the field of adult education would result from an in-depth examination of adult education agencies, associations, and institutions. However, it quickly became apparent that there are few organizations devoted solely to adult education, so that an attempt to study those few would result in neglect of the bulk of the activities and processes we normally associate with adult education. Therefore, this volume is concerned with the whole range of adult education enterprises, regardless of their organizational base.

At present, adult education has no single rallying point strong enough to bring an essential unity to the field. There is considerable concern, however, among professional adult educators about the fragmentation of adult education, the lack of broad leadership in the field, and a possible con- comitant loss of professional identity. (Other fields, including social work, health care delivery, and criminology, face simi- lar concerns.) A search for order in adult education thus appears justified. The authors of this volume approach their work from individual points of view, but they all share "sys- tems thinking"—the ability to see the whole of adult educa- tion rather than to approach it from a narrow perspective. This breadth is essential to the examination of a field as broad and complex as adult education. The systems approach must have few exceptions, and it must be firmly anchored in the nature of human behavior. It must not be institution specific or biased by a particular organizational contrivance; instead it must transcend the limits imposed by specific arrangements of properties inherent in agencies, institutions, and associa- tions. The systems approach should reflect a way of thinking about organized forms of behavior so as to guide thought rather than to restrict it to parameters imposed by particular applications. The reader is encouraged to "step back" a few paces from the ocean of enterprises of adult education, ex- amine the ebb and flow of its forms and processes, and join the authors in their search for order and meaning in a field that Bryson (1936) found to "express the complexity and vitality of life." The reader will have several knowledgeable guides in the inquiry into the organization of adult education. Malcolm Knowles reviews the growth and development of adult education and reflects on contemporary organizational forms. Wayne Schroeder painstakingly orders the field in terms of its systems and types. William Griffith examines the issue of coordinating adult education both in the United States and abroad. I consider the promise of a systems per- spective for the study of adult education organizations. Finally, Owen McCullough provides an overview of what he labels "creative anarchy." The introductory chapter is designed to provide a framework for considering each of these approaches.

I was not alone in the struggle to fit these pieces together into a coherent, comprehensive treatment of the organization of adult education. Any degree of success is due precisely to the superior work of the authors and all the others who labored so diligently and patiently to turn out this volume. My colleagues at the University of British Columbia, where I began the work of putting this book together, and my students and colleagues at the University of Tennessee, where I completed it, deserve praise for their support. On behalf of the authors, I acknowledge all the people in their professional and personal lives who supported their labors on behalf of the Adult Education Association of the U.S.A.

Knoxville, Tennessee   JOHN M. PETERS
February 1980

Contents

The Authors

WILLIAM S. GRIFFITH, professor of adult education, University of British Columbia

MALCOLM S. KNOWLES, national lecturer in learning theory, Nova University

CHARLES P. KOZOLL, associate director for program development, Office of Continuing Education and Public Service, University of Illinois

K. OWEN McCULLOUGH, associate professor of continuing and higher education, University of Tennessee

JOHN M. PETERS, professor of continuing and higher education, University of Tennessee

WAYNE L. SCHROEDER, professor of adult education, Florida State University

Building
an Effective
Adult Education
Enterprise

Chapter One

Organization of the Field

John M. Peters
Charles P. Kozoll

Adult education can be characterized as an amorphous, hybrid field, comprised of a variety of domestic and international components. Its clientele are as varied as the entire adult population, and its methods include all the arrangements between learner and mentor ever contrived by pedagogists and andragogists alike. Adult education activities take place in organizations with both primary and lesser interest in education, in a manner more diverse than youth education. The majority of adult education activities take place in institutions that are not primarily intended for adult education purposes: museums, libraries, social agencies, voluntary associations, churches, industrial organizations, labor unions, professional societies, and governments at all levels. Those

1

institutions created primarily for the education of adults—such as proprietary schools and independent adult education centers—are far fewer in number.

Although adult education has moved further into the informal processes than into the formal structures of institutions, almost all forms of organized human behavior include adult education aspects. Moreover, because adult education somehow relates to all established institutions, viewing the field in terms of organizations has become a favorite practice of scholars interested in discovering order amid the diversity. Whether this affinity for organizational frameworks is due to a lack of a satisfactory alternate form of identification or to a failure to probe for the underpinnings of adult education is unclear. Nevertheless, existing formal organizations represent the need of a society for social organization, and evolving structures of adult education tend to vary with society's needs and its array of functions. In this chapter we shall show the inadequacy of the current organizational typologies and then describe how the use of systems thinking can be employed to explain major organizational and interorganizational phenomena. The chapters that follow serve as effective demonstrations of the use of systems thinking in adult education.

In Search of Order

The need for an organizational typology prompted Schroeder (1970, pp. 37–38) to adapt from the work of Houle (1964) and Verner and Booth (1964) the following types of agencies in adult education:

- Type I Agencies, established to serve the educational needs of adults—adult education is a central function.
- Type II Agencies, established to serve the educational needs of youth which have assumed the added responsibility of at least partially serving the educational needs of adults—adult education is a secondary function.
- Type III Agencies, established to serve both educational and non-educational needs of the community—adult edu-

cation is an allied function employed to fulfill only some of the needs which agencies recognize as their responsibility.
- Type IV Agencies, established to serve the special interests of special groups—adult education is a subordinate function employed primarily to further the interests of the agency itself.

Type I agencies are exemplified by proprietary schools and independent residential and nonresidential centers. Type II agencies include (among others) the public schools and colleges and universities. Libraries and museums typify Type III agencies, and examples of Type IV agencies are business and industry, labor unions, government, churches, and voluntary associations. Schroeder's characterization of adult education in terms of agency types is further developed in Chapter Three of this volume.

A less direct way of understanding how adult education is organized is by examining the basic forms of organization within which adult education activities are developed and implemented. This involves the use of organizational models or conceptualizations, which are said to depict the several ways in which people may be organized to accomplish work. Primarily the product of sociologists, political scientists, and organization theorists, models serve as frameworks for inquiry into the complexities of organized forms of human behavior. Their use in the study of adult education, however, has been quite limited.

Rice and Bishoprick (1971) have summarized seven conceptual models of organizations, useful to anyone who seeks a better understanding of the way in which people organize to achieve society's purposes. They are distributed along a continuum that runs the gamut from autocratic to egalitarian, with bureaucracies, collegial organizations, federations, and decentralized forms of organizations at the center. The military, government, business, and industry can be found on one side of the continuum, with higher education and professional associations generally found on the other—though the distinctions are not always clear. The former group may be authority concentrated, relate more closely to McGregor's (1960) Theory X, and be more coercive in nature. Those on the right side of the continuum are likely to be democratically managed, have more equally distributed authority, and be ruled by custom.

It is easy enough to find an example of each organizational form among the several types of institutions, agencies, and associations that have adult education as one of their functions. It is more difficult to classify "Type I Agencies" in such a fashion. With few exceptions, therefore, the models are more helpful in understanding how organizations function in general than in understanding the distinct ways in which adult education is organized. Moreover, adult education activities are particularly difficult to fit into established forms, because they cut across institutional lines. Adult education practitioners not only operate within established organizations but also work outside them as catalysts between organizations, within informal groups, and as individuals. Add to this Schroeder's conceptualization of adult education as "a process that links various agent and client systems . . . to produce program decisions" (Chapter Three) and it becomes impossible to classify such diverse areas of practice using conventional models of organization as a framework for analysis.

An adequate conceptualization of an area of practice so broad and varied as adult education requires a framework that depicts organized forms of behavior that are not tied to a particular institution or type of formal organization. The conceptualization must incorporate processes as well as structures, and its scope must have enough range to include the relationships among the diverse ways adult education is organized. The framework should allow for the integration of the several forms and activities in the field so as to provide a basis for charting a common direction for the enterprises of adult education. In short, the framework should represent a way of thinking about organized forms of behavior that can guide inquiry into the nature of a specific area of practice such as adult education. One such framework requires the adoption of a systems perspective.

Maccoby (1976) characterized a corporate leader as

having a "systems mind" because he always saw details in terms of an overall picture. Systems thinking allows one to see the whole and not merely the parts, and includes the ability to integrate many ideas into an overall plan. This depiction of one style of thinking illustrates the approach suggested in this chapter. To gain a perspective on the whole of adult education requires systems thinking. General systems theory offers the raw material for developing such a mode of thought. The following brief review of some of the concepts and propositions inherent in this relatively new area of study should enhance our inquiry into the way adult education is organized.

Defining Systems

Webster's 1972 dictionary defines a system as "an organized or complex whole . . . an assemblage or combination of things or parts forming a complex or unitary whole." Optner (1965, p. 26) defines a system as "an on-going process . . . anything in motion, in process, or in a state of change." Ackoff (1960, p. 1) views a system as "any entity, conceptual or physical, which consists of interdependent parts." Rice and Bishoprick (1971, p. 163) add that "a system consists of a patterned, functioning relationship among components." Boulding (1956, p. 12) advocated a "spectrum of theories . . . a system of systems which may perform the function of a gestalt in theoretical construction." This attempt toward wholeness and resolution of common concerns of the several disciplines has generated a number of useful concepts for emerging areas of inquiry such as adult education.

Systems theory deals with properties, structures, functions, and processes of living systems. Theoretical statements, such as those related to living organisms, have utility for generating theory about social organizations with open systems characteristics. Griffiths (1964) noted the utility of systems theory in social systems analysis in explaining and predicting a wide range of human behavior within organizations. There is a high degree of correspondence between the concept of social systems—or the manner of conceiving human organization in terms of structure, function, and process—and the way in which biologists and psychologists have conceived them as open organismic systems (Hearn, 1958). Formal organizations, communities, societies, and certain informal groups are examples of open systems. They are also the substance and vehicles for the organization and delivery of adult education processes.

Thousands of different systems exist in contemporary society. They vary in complexity from multinational corporations to a single classroom in a rural area where adults prepare for a high school equivalency examination. Obviously, the products of the two extremes differ a great deal. In adult education, a principle product (or output, in systems terminology) is increased competency of the adult learner who participates in educational programs (Knox, 1967). Moreover, the process that links various agent and client systems to produce program decisions is also a system that can be analyzed in terms of properties common to all systems.

Utility and Application of Systems Concepts

Concepts derived from systems theory are useful to the study of the organization of adult education, and for this volume they provide a context in which to analyze the several chapters and to link the complementary areas of adult education each author examines. Few of the authors deal with specific systems concepts, but their ways of thinking about the field represent a holistic and comprehensive approach to characterizing its elements and processes. It is easy to detect their tendencies in this direction, even though there are instances in which they reflect doubts we all share occasionally about the presence of a true system of adult education. The following overview of the chapters in this book should illustrate our belief in the utility of a systems framework for examining the organization of adult education.

In Chapter Two, Knowles argues that adult education is not organized in the sense of being formed into a coherent unity or functioning whole but is instead a complex mosaic of unrelated activities or processes. Comparing Knowles' characterization with the definitions of systems, the casual reader may be left with the distinct impression that no system of adult education exists—at least not in the strict organizational sense. However, Knowles allows room for further systems analysis when he depicts adult education as permeating almost all of the established organizations of society and when he discusses a new emerging educational system.

Knowles believes that the lack of unity and coherence that characterized the early years of adult education was largely due to (1) the reactive nature of adult education programming; (2) the development of adult education units as adjuncts of established systems rather than as discrete, independent organizations; and (3) the development of individual and agency loyalties to specialized interests and aims. The very survival of organized forms of adult education seemed to depend on the extent that they were imbedded in organizations with a primary purpose other than adult education. However, some new developments have occurred more recently that promise greater unity and coherence in the field.

One of the best examples of organizational development in favor of unity in the field as practiced in the United States was the establishment in 1926 of the American Association for Adult Education (and in 1951 its successor, the Adult Education Association of the U.S.A.). The aims of these organizations included the development of national goals and directions for the field of adult education. In 1969, the Coalition of Adult Education Organizations formed to provide greater unity among more than a dozen major associations involved in adult education. Griffith (Chapter Four) details these and other state, local, and international efforts to establish unity through improved coordination of adult education.

Knowles makes two fundamental assumptions about the evolving structure of adult education that signal possible new and better-organized forms of adult education. One assumption is that adult education programs tend to gain

stability and permanence as they become increasingly differential in administration, finance, curriculum, and methodology. This assumption is consistent with the maturation
process that typifies systems in general. The stronger subsystems and related functions are, the greater the likelihood
that their parent systems will survive and prosper—a point
more fully developed in Chapter Five of this volume. It is also
consistent with what we know about the increasing strength
and importance of such organized forms of adult education
as divisions of continuing education in colleges and
universities.

Another of Knowles' assumptions is that the field of
adult education is beginning to reflect many of the universal
elements and processes of social systems. This characteristic is
illustrated by citing the interactive qualities of segments of
the field. In another publication, Knowles (1967) cites the
relationships of specialists who work within the same content
areas but are employed by different agencies in different
geographic areas. Home economists, for example, are employed by the Cooperative Extension Service, private
industry, the public schools, and higher education institutions. They share a common professional interest in the education of adults, and they interact on a local, regional, and
national scale. Thus, they effectively develop a form of interorganizational relationship, providing in Knowles'
framework a profile of adult education as a social system.

Whether Knowles is correct in his observation that the
entire field is evolving as a social system remains for the
future to reveal. One thing is clear, however, from the facts
cited in Chapter Two: There are increasing numbers and
varieties of adult education, and inasmuch as these forms are
called organizations of adult education, they are indeed social
systems.

If a system of adult education is evolving, it would
necessarily exhibit the qualities of wholeness and order. It is
in pursuit of order that Schroeder (Chapter Three) develops
a typology of organized forms of adult education. His typology is an attempt to provide a framework within which to

examine the complexities of the evolving structure of the field. Schroeder views the field as "a process used to link various agent and client systems together for the purpose of establishing directions and procedures for programs of adult learning." His approach clearly reflects a systems way of thinking.

Schroeder's "process" refers to the decisions that result in the identification and organization of major program components, including needs, objectives, and procedures. Importantly, it is the interaction and special influences of the two macro systems (agent and client) that give birth to adult education program structure and operations. Comprehending the process system of adult education therefore requires that it be studied with reference to its environment, both internal and external, and with regard to the reciprocal effects each has on the other. Schroeder's classification provides a focus on the way adult education systems may interact with client systems to produce programs having a variety of orientations. These orientations may be client centered, agent centered, or a combination of both.

Schroeder's major contribution to the literature is his development of a new perspective on the structure of adult education. In Schroeder's opinion, his classification system will "help practitioners become more discriminating in their use of knowledge and researchers more realistic and generative in their search for knowledge." We believe Schroeder's chapter is a work whose timeliness is one of its greatest strengths.

In Chapter Four, Griffith treats the problem of coordination of organized forms of adult education. Although the problem is often a philosophical issue, Griffith places it in perspective with his claim that if adult education is to become more than the sum of its individual components, adult educators will have to address the question of its coordination His illustrations, drawn from several countries, amplify the concern for coordination.

The problem of coordination of adult education is ironically a product of its own maturation. Though we have never had a coordinated field of operations, rapid growth in the modern era has drastically increased the need for coordination of its parts. The growth of systems quite naturally leads to such a state as they require meaningful interaction among their parts and as these parts gain in strength.

One hallmark of a discipline is its ability to produce and use its own knowledge base. People in the field of adult education who value a disciplinary orientation appreciate the critical role of research and theory development in the maturation of a new field of inquiry. In Chapter Five, Peters further develops the systems theme and describes the role systems theory might play in our attempt to understand more adequately the structure of adult education. Peters does not take a position on the matter of whether a system of adult education does indeed exist. Rather, he suggests various conceptual tools the reader might use to develop a profile of individual and multiple systems that sponsor adult education programs in order to decide whether the object of analysis can be called a system. Peters' example of the Adult Education Association of the U.S.A. as a system is meant to illustrate the approach he recommends.

It should be apparent by now that we have suggested a systems way of thinking about the evolving structure of adult education. The reader who requires more information about systems to appreciate our argument for a systems view will find that information in Chapter Five.

In Chapter Six, McCullough offers a critique of the first five chapters in the hope of stimulating the reader's thinking about the nature of the evolving structure of adult education. McCullough also shares his own point of view regarding the field and identifies one of the major contributions made by this book: It opens an area of inquiry into the structure of the field and invites scholars and practitioners alike to build on this base as they develop their own understanding of adult education.

As has been mentioned previously, the authors were not instructed to utilize systems theory concepts in developing their chapters. However, their years of practice and study in the field have led to their development of a broad under-standing of the underpinnings and universalities of the field. Consequently it is not surprising that their writing reflects the same broad perspective that characterizes systems thinking. Readers are encouraged to follow the authors' example—to step back mentally to view the full range of adult education and to develop their own conception of the building of the adult education enterprise.

Chapter Two

The Growth and Development of Adult Education

Malcolm S. Knowles

Any attempt to understand the organizational arrangements of adult education in the United States by analogy—comparing them with other kinds of organizations—is fraught with difficulties. Adult education in this country is not "organized" in the dictionary sense of being formed into a coherent unity or functioning whole. It is a complex mosaic of unrelated activities and processes that permeate almost all the established organizations in our society.

As early as 1936, Bryson had this insight about adult education:

> American adult education has not been of a single and systematic character. . . . It has always been carried on by a wide variety of agencies, for a variety of purposes, and with many different kinds of

people. For this reason, some critics have called it
formless and without direction. Actually it has penetrated to more phases of life in America than in any
other country. It has been thoroughly in accord with
our basic democratic idea that education is a common
right, that learning is neither something reserved for
an aristocracy nor something bequeathed by a
superior class to inferiors. Most American adult education enterprises have been organized voluntarily,
even when carried on under public auspices. They
have expressed the complexity and vitality of American Life [1936, pp. 13–14].

The term *adult education* has been used in the literature
with three different meanings: (1) a field of operations that
encompasses all the organized activities in which mature men
and women engage for the purpose of learning, usually
under the auspices of an institution; (2) a process of self-
directed inquiry through which individuals systematically
learn from their daily experiences and other resources in
their environment; and (3) a social movement that encompasses the whole spectrum of mature individuals learning in
infinite ways under innumerable auspices the many things
that make life richer and more civilized and is dedicated to
the improvement of the process of adult learning, the extension of opportunities for adults to learn, and the advancement of the general level of our culture. As we shall see,
organizational patterns have evolved around all three of
these meanings. These organizational patterns will be
examined through a brief historical overview and an analysis
of major forces and developments in the modern era.

Early Processes and Institutions

Adult education might be said to have begun in the
United States when the early settlers learned from the In-
dians how to grow corn, conquer the elements, and survive in
the inhospitable New World. Another example of adult education—one of the most important in our history—occurred
during the colonial period, when the colonists were learning

to use the tools of liberty and self-government through participation in town meetings, colonial legislatures, and other governmental activities. Probably no social undertaking ever staked more on the ability of adults to learn than did the founding of the republic, for the new government could survive only if it succeeded in transforming, in one generation, an entire people from subjects to citizens—from a people accustomed to being governed by an aristocracy to a people able to govern themselves. The methods by which this enormous adult education task was accomplished were informal, unorganized, and in a sense unconscious. They included town meetings, cracker-barrel discussions, correspondence, pamphlets, editorials, books, speeches, poems, and plays, all of which explored the issues and ideas of democracy. Although the American Revolution was one of the most significant political revolutions in history, it was an equally significant social and intellectual revolution.

At about the time that the "Common Man" was mastering the new role of citizen-ruler, the world was being illuminated by the dawn of the age of science. In the years between the Revolution and the Civil War, there was an upsurge of secular thought and interest in natural science, producing an unprecedented hunger for knowledge. This urge for the diffusion of knowledge expressed itself in many ways. Numerous institutions were founded during this period, including the American Academy of Arts and Sciences (1780), the Pennsylvania Academy of Fine Arts (1791), the Boston Mechanics Institute (1826), the Franklin Institute in New Haven (1828), the Lowell Institute in Boston (1836), the Smithsonian Institution in Washington (1846), the first public library in Boston (1848), the Y.M.C.A. (1851), Cooper Union in New York City (1859), the land grant colleges (established by the Morrill Act of 1862), and the first women's club (1866).

The first and one of the most famous national adult education programs, the American Lyceum, was also organized during this period. Founded in 1831 by Josiah Holbrook of Massachusetts, the Lyceum flourished until by

1835 there were some 3,000 town lyceums presenting weekly lecture-discussions for the mutual improvement of their members and the common benefit of society. Their principal project was the advancement of the public school movement. By 1845, the Lyceum had largely accomplished its purpose and rapidly disappeared from the scene. But it had developed a form of education—the lecture-discussion—which was later to be adopted and extended by successors such as the Chautauqua, university extension, and public forum movements.

The dominating spirit of the adult education movement up to the Civil War was the diffusion of knowledge; that of the period between the Civil War and World War I might be characterized as the diffusion of organizations. During this period, the penchant for "joining," which de Tocqueville had observed in Americans in the 1830s, reached its full force. Hardly a year passed without the founding of several organizations concerned with social or individual self-improvement. Most institutions that provide educational opportunities for adults trace their birth to this era.

One of the brightest stars in adult education skies in these years was the Chautauqua Institution. Established in 1874 in Chautauqua, New York, as a summer school for Sunday School teachers, Chautauqua rapidly broadened its program to include literature, science, history, and other subjects of general culture. Its Literary and Scientific Circle, which was founded in 1878 and grew into a nationwide system of home study carried on in connection with local reading circles, popularized a new adult education form, the correspondence course. For many years the traveling Chautauquas (inspired but not sponsored by Chautauqua Institution) carried cultural stimulation into the byways of rural America.

The middle 1800s also witnessed the founding of myriad welfare agencies, including settlement houses; the Salvation Army; family welfare societies; youth agencies such as the YMCA, YWCA, YWHA, Boy Scouts, Girl Scouts, and Campfire Girls; fraternal organizations such as Rotary, Kiwanis, Altrusa, and Lions; and health agencies such as the

National Tuberculosis Association, the American Social Hygiene Association, and the Red Cross. All of these are concerned with the education of adults as volunteers, members, or clients. During this period there was also a phenomenal growth of large-scale voluntary associations with primarily adult educational purposes, such as the National Congress of Parents and Teachers, the General Federation of Women's Clubs, the American Association of University Women, the National Council of Jewish Women, B'nai B'rith, and many others. Labor unions, manufacturers' associations, trade associations, and other groups were organized around economic interests to promote the education of their members and the public.

One of the most popular and far-reaching innovations of this time was the idea of systematic learning by correspondence. Pioneered by the Chautauqua Institution, the idea was rapidly developed by private correspondence schools, the largest and best known of which is the International Correspondence Schools, founded in Scranton, Pennsylvania, in 1891. Many universities adopted the idea and established home-study departments. Since then, millions of American citizens have received further education by correspondence.

The established educational institutions—the public schools, colleges, and universities—also developed extensive adult education programs during the middle 1880s. While evening classes for adults had been instituted in a few scattered communities before the Civil War, the evening school did not become an established part of the public school program until the massive waves of immigration later in the century created a serious problem of "Americanization." In 1889, an appropriation of $15,000 was included in the regular budget for evening lectures in New York City schools for the first time. By World War I, statewide systems of evening schools, with continuous state assistance, began to appear. The idea that a university is responsible for educating the adult citizens of its community smoldered for half a century before bursting into a blaze of extension departments around the turn of the century. The University of the State of New York received the first state appropriation for university extension in 1891, and the first national conference on university extension was held in the same year. At the founding of the University of Chicago in 1892, university extension was included as a formal, permanent division of the university. The modern model of university extension was created at the University of Wisconsin in 1906, when emphasis was shifted from academic and cultural subjects to an all-embracing concept of service that covered, in addition to those subjects, all subjects concerned with the problems of the people and the state—agricultural, industrial, political, social, and moral. Following this broad pattern, extension divisions have been organized in the majority of colleges and universities of the country.

Another development at the turn of the century that has affected the character of the adult education movement in this country to the present time was the gathering of leaders of adult education into associations according to type of institution, occupational interest, or type of subject matter for the purpose of promoting the advancement of their particular interests. Examples of these early associations are the American Public Health Association, the American Library Association, the Association of Land Grant Colleges and Universities, the National University Extension Association, and the American Home Economics Association. Although most of these associations were not concerned exclusively with adult education and did not call it by that name, it was an important phase of their work.

Two significant patterns in the early organization of the adult education movement stand out: (1) Adult education developed as an adjunct of some other kind of activity rather than as a discrete activity with independent character. (2) Individuals and agencies concerned with the education of adults developed communication and loyalties in specialized interest areas before there was any consciousness of common national aims. The emerging pattern of growth of the adult education movement thus became a designless mosaic, rich in diversity but devoid of unity.

The Modern Era

Following the advent of the First World War, the modern era of adult education began. A number of new forces pushed the adult education movement in new directions, and a number of old forces were strengthened.

On the local level, the impulse toward coordination and cooperation expressed itself with the organization during the 1930s of several dozen local, state, and regional adult education councils. Almost all of them sponsored conferences, information exchanges, directories of agencies, and newsletters. Some of them also conducted surveys of community needs, maintained counseling services, stimulated joint planning, sponsored training programs, promoted community-wide publicity campaigns, and operated experimental programs. Few of the local councils survived into the 1970s (see Chapter Four for more detail). In fact, many of the functions of the local councils were beginning to be performed in the 1970s by the rapidly expanding community school and educational brokerage agency movements, which are discussed later in this chapter.

The Changing Role of Government

One of the most powerful new forces was the direct support by the federal government of certain phases of adult education. The dam had been broken with the passage in 1914 of the Smith-Lever Act, which provided federal funds to augment state funds for the establishment and operation of a cooperative agricultural extension service. Over the years, this program has grown to be one of the largest single enterprises in adult education. By the middle of this century there were 12,000 county agents, home demonstration agents, and subject matter specialists who influenced almost seven million farm families with some phase of extension work. The agricultural extension service, reinforced by several thousand vocational agriculture teachers in rural public schools and by general social progress, has probably made more of an impact on a national culture than any other social force in history. During the first forty years of its existence, revolutionary advances took place not only in farming habits but also in such aspects of living as childraising, food selection and preparation, health practices, and cultural activities of rural families. Without doubt many of these changes have been wrought by the automobile, radio, refrigerator, and other technological improvements. But the speed, smoothness, and universality with which these changes have taken place are testimony that adult education can make a difference.

The federal government next moved into the field of adult education in response to the need for skilled industrial workers in war industries. The Smith-Hughes Act, passed in 1917, made federal funds available to augment state and local funds for the expansion of vocational education in agriculture and the mechanical arts, principally through the public schools. These funds were augmented further during the Depression of the 1930s by the passage of the George-Deen Act. The Depression witnessed further support for adult education by the federal government through a wide variety of activities by the Works Progress Administration, the National Youth Administration, and the Civilian Conservation Corps. The government also provided one of the most dramatic examples of community adult education through the work of the Tennessee Valley Authority. In a sense, the G.I. Bill following World War II was also an instance of direct federal support of adult education.

Following a lull in activity during the 1950s, the federal government took a historical turn in the early 1960s in providing legislation, financial support, and policy leadership to education in general. In regard to adult education, the initial federal thrust was on providing training to unemployed heads of households who had previous employment experience. The Area Redevelopment Act (1961) and the Manpower Development and Training Act (1962) sought to aid those persons whose unemployment was caused by geographic shifts in the demand for labor and changes in skill requirements resulting from technological advances.

By 1964, although the general employment picture

was improving, disproportionately high percentages of unemployment remained for blacks, non-English-speaking adults, and the undereducated. With the passage of the Economic Opportunity Act of 1964, the Adult Basic Education program was established. This program sought to remedy the inequities of educational disadvantage by offering people 18 years of age and older the opportunity to develop reading, writing, language, and mathematical skills to enable them to obtain employment. The Office of Economic Opportunity provided funds to the U.S. Office of Education to administer the program until the Adult Education Act of 1966 (Title III of the 1966 Amendments to the Elementary and Secondary Education Act—P.L. 89-750) placed the program entirely within the U.S. Office of Education.

     Under this landmark act, adult basic and secondary educational programs were established in each of the states and territories. Funds were available to state and local education agencies to meet the costs of instruction, to employ and train qualified adult educators, and to develop specialized curricula and techniques appropriate for adult learners. Enrollments in programs under the Adult Education Act increased from 37,991 in fiscal year 1965 to almost one million in fiscal year 1974. (For a detailed description of these acts and programs, see National Advisory Council on Adult Education, 1974.)

     The original Adult Education Act in 1966 established an eight-member Advisory Committee on Adult Basic Education, which in the 1970 amendments was enlarged to a fifteen-member National Advisory Council with the following responsibilities: (1) advising the Commissioner of Education in the preparation of general regulations; (2) advising the commissioner with respect to policies and procedures governing state plans and policies to eliminate duplication; (3) advising the commissioner with respect to coordination of programs offering adult education activities and services; (4) reviewing the administration and effectiveness of programs; and (5) making annual reports to the president of findings and recommendations relating to adult education activities and services. For the first time in history, the federal government had established a national body with authority to influence national policy regarding adult education. During the next five years, the National Advisory Council conducted studies, held regional meetings of leaders in adult education, and published findings and recommendations which in fact did affect legislation and programs (National Advisory Council on Adult Education, 1971).

The 1970 amendments to the Adult Education Act (P.L. 91-23) authorized the establishment of state advisory councils on adult education with the hope of providing the same policy leadership for state governments that the National Advisory Council had demonstrated at the federal level. In 1975, the National Advisory Council made a survey of state councils and found that: "twenty-six state advisory councils for adult education are now in existence, although two are not operational. Twenty-three states and territories indicated no councils and no plans to establish one. Six states indicated that their councils are combined in some way with vocational, technical, or community education" (National Advisory Council on Adult Education, 1976). The prevailing sentiment appeared to be one of resistance to councils whose membership was mandated by the federal government.

Research, statistical publications, and advisory services to the field of adult education by the federal government were greatly strengthened and expanded during the 1960s with the establishment of several new agencies. For example, the National Center for Education Statistics (NCES) was created within the U.S. Office of Education in 1965 with a congressional mandate to collect statistics and facts to show the condition and progress of education in the states and territories. Its regular publications in adult education include reports on participation of adults in educational programs sponsored by higher education institutions, public education systems, and community organizations. There appeared to be some hope during the 1960s that the statistical jungle of adult education could become civilized. The Educational Resources Information Center (ERIC) was established in the

Office of Education at about the same time as NCES and in 1973 was moved to the newly created National Institute for Education. As a part of this reorganization, the Clearinghouse in Adult Education, originally situated at Syracuse University, was moved to Northern Illinois University and joined with the Clearinghouse in Career Education. In 1976 this joint clearinghouse was moved to Ohio State University. One of a network of sixteen clearinghouses, the Clearinghouse in Career Education collects computerized data from journal articles, significant project reports, research reports, curriculum guides, bibliographies, survey results, speeches, conference proceedings, and other sources.

In-service education for governmental employees continued to expand in keeping with the policy guidelines of the Government Employees Training Act of 1958 and leadership from the Civil Service Commission. By 1976, almost 750,000 civilian employees were reached through eighty-three agency-operated centers, the National Independent Study Center (opened by the Civil Service Commission in 1976), and 120 off-campus study centers in cooperation with colleges and universities. Another third of a million military personnel participated in a variety of training programs conducted by the Department of Defense (U.S. Civil Service Commission, 1976).

Numerous federal agencies—including the Public Health Service, the National Park Service, the National Endowment for the Humanities, the National Science Foundation, the Office of Consumer Affairs, and the Bureau of Indian Affairs—continued to provide educational programs and services to selected segments of the public. State governments also enlarged their role in adult education during this period; by 1970, adult education offices with full-time directors had been established in the education departments in all fifty states and Puerto Rico.

National Organization

A second force that influenced the modern era was the pressure toward national integration of adult education activities. Until 1924, the term *adult education* was practically unknown in this country; agencies engaged in educating adults were so unrelated they did not even have a common name for what they were doing. But in that year Frederick P. Keppel, the newly elected president of the Carnegie Corporation of New York, returned from an inspection of the national adult education movements of Europe with a vision of an integrated movement in this country. Under his leadership, a series of conferences was held with leaders of various agencies, resulting in the founding in 1926 of the American Association for Adult Education. During its twenty-five years of existence, the association served as a national clearinghouse for information about adult education. It conducted annual conferences, published a quarterly journal of adult education (1929–1951), sponsored many studies, and published a large library of books, the most notable of which was the series *Studies in the Social Significance of Adult Education.* The association was generously financed by the Carnegie Corporation during most of its life and was further supported by modest dues from about 3,000 members.

Five years before the founding of the American Association for Adult Education, a Department of Immigrant Education had been established in the National Education Association. Originally composed of administrators and teachers of programs for the foreign born, the department gradually broadened its scope and in 1924 changed its name to the Department of Adult Education. For several years its members were drawn exclusively from the public school field, but in 1927 it amended its constitution to permit any person engaged in teaching, supervising, or administering programs of adult education, under public or private auspices, to join. During the 1930s and 1940s many people from outside the public school field joined the department, participated in its conferences, received its bimonthly *Adult Education Bulletin,* and obtained other services.

By 1941, the purposes, programs, and memberships of these two national organizations overlapped to such a degree that strong sentiment existed for uniting them into a single national organization. A joint committee of the two

organizations conducted a series of conferences that resulted
in the decision to dissolve both organizations and to create a
totally new, unifying national organization. As a result, the
Adult Education Association of the U.S.A. was founded at an
assembly of over 200 leaders of adult education at Columbus,
Ohio, on May 14, 1951. The purpose and structure of the
Adult Education Association are discussed by Peters in Chapter Five of this volume.

The NEA's Department of Adult Education (a membership unit) changed its status in 1968 to that of a National
Affiliate of the NEA under its new name, National Association for Public School Adult Education (NAPSAE). As discussed by Griffith in Chapter Four, NAPSAE has since
changed its name to the National Association for Public Continuing and Adult Education.

The urge to bring greater unity and coherence to the
field of adult education gained its most visible expression
with the convening in December 1969 of a Galaxy Conference of Adult Education Organizations in Washington, D.C.
The notion of having a number of the national organizations
in the field hold their annual meetings simultaneously in the
same city, so that they could come together for some joint
sessions, evolved from a meeting of the leaders of seventeen
organizations who convened at Syracuse University in 1964
to discuss the creation of its Library of Continuing Education. As a result of these discussions, a Committee of Adult
Education Organizations was formed in 1966 to plan the
Galaxy Conference in 1969.

A total of 2,508 representatives of twenty organizations attended the Galaxy Conference; eight of them held
their annual meetings there. They took two actions subject to
later ratification by their respective organizations: (1) the
adoption of "Imperatives for Action," a statement of goals
for the adult education movement, and (2) the adoption of a
constitution for a new organization, the Coalition of Adult
Education Organizations (CAEO).

The constitution of the CAEO stated that "the overall
purpose of the Coalition is to provide a basis for cooperation

and action among the several organizations and associations in promoting adult and continuing education." (The specific purposes of CAEO are discussed in Chapter Four.) By 1976, the CAEO had grown to include nineteen member organizations and one associate member, representing diverse elements of the field; they are: the Adult Education Association of the U.S.A.; Adult Student Personnel Association; American Library Association; American Association of Community and Junior Colleges; American Society for Training and Development; Association for Continuing Higher Education; Association for Continuing Professional Education; Institute of Lifetime Learning; Library of Continuing Education, Syracuse University; National Association of Black Adult Educators; National Association for Public Continuing and Adult Education; National Community Education Association; National Council of Churches; National Council on Community Services and Continuing Education; National Education Association; National Home Study Council; National University Extension Association; United States Association of Evening Students; University and College Labor Education Association; National Multimedia Center for Adult Education/National Adult Education Clearinghouse (associate member).

Foundation Support

Another force influencing adult education in the modern era has been large-scale support by private foundations. The pace was set by the Carnegie Corporation of New York, with its financing of the American Association for Adult Education. While it supported the basic organizational services of the association, the Carnegie Corporation's major emphasis was on the development of a body of adult education literature. Many of the classics in the present literature were made possible by Carnegie grants. The Kellogg Foundation has also been active in supporting special projects, notably Centers for Continuing Education at Michigan State University, the University of Georgia, the University of

Nebraska, the University of Chicago, Notre Dame University, Columbia University, the University of New Hampshire, Oxford University, California Polytechnic State College, and The Fund for Adult Education, Utah State University, made available large sums between 1951 and 1961 for the support of the Adult Education Association of the U.S.A., the expansion of liberal education programs such as the Great Books Program, the development of educational television, the promotion of film-discussion projects, and the general furtherance of liberal adult education. The Mott Foundation of Flint, Michigan, has been the chief source of support for the rapidly expanding community school movement.

Business and Industry

Various institutional settings have responded in a number of ways to external and internal social forces affecting adult education. For example, factors such as the growth in the number and size of corporations, the increasing professionalization of management, and the acceleration of technological change have resulted in the emergence of corporate training and management development as one of the major educational enterprises of the country. In an increasing number of firms, the training function has been upgraded to the larger concept of "human resources development," and its status has been raised from a secondary function of personnel departments to separate departments reporting directly to top management. The size of training staffs has increased proportionately. For example, the membership of the American Society for Training and Development, which represents only a small fraction of training personnel, grew from around 4,000 in 1960 to over 10,000 in 1976.

A new institutional form—the private consulting firm specializing in training—has emerged and flourished. The Consultant Directory published in the *Training and Development Journal* in 1972 contained 190 listings of these firms. The American Management Associations' seminars and institutes for supervisors and executives, which could be described in a small brochure in the early 1960s, required a large catalog in the late 1970s.

Another institutional form that has mushroomed is the corporate residential training center, such as General Electric's Management Development Institute at Crotonville, New York, and the IBM Management Center at Sands Point, Long Island. The General Motors Institute in Flint, Michigan, has even been accredited to award academic degrees. No comprehensive listing of corporate training centers has been developed, but several hundred of them must have been established by 1979.

A closely related new institutional form is the commercial conference center, such as the Harrison Houses on Long Island and in Lake Bluff, Illinois, and Arlie House in Virginia. In addition to residential facilities and meeting rooms, these centers provide elaborate media, administrative support, and consultation services. They are heavily used by corporations, business and professional associations, and government agencies.

Colleges and Universities

The modern era has witnessed an explosive growth in the expansion of higher education—in terms of both size and scope of services. Notable growth has occurred in continuing professional development activities for physicians, nurses, engineers, teachers, and other professional groups, including the establishment of extension centers in remote areas of the country and the creation of statewide networks of dial-access information retrieval systems and computer-assisted instruction. Extension curriculums have become increasingly organized around the life concerns of adult learners, and teaching strategies have increasingly engaged the adult learners in planning and supervising their own learning. Administrative responsibility for continuing education has become more centralized and elevated in the university hierarchy, with many universities elevating the office of dean of extension to

that of vice president or vice chancellor. Extension staffs have
grown in size, stature, and differentiation of role; and an
increasing number of position announcements specify that a
doctorate in adult education is a prerequisite. Budgetary allo-
cations for continuing education have increased—both absolutely and in relation to the budgets of other units of the
universities—and the income from extension activities has
become an increasingly important factor in the economic
health of many institutions of higher education. Following
the example of the Kellogg Centers for Continuing Education, most of the larger universities in the country have
established continuing education centers (some residential,
some nonresidential) designed expressly for the education of
adults. Enrollments in university extension increased, according to the Bureau of the Census, from 843,923 in 1952 to
3,367,000 in 1972 (National Center for Education Statistics,
1975, p. 136).

　　A number of forces peculiar to the modern era were
exerting pressure on institutions of higher education to
expand and change their services to adult learners. Nine of
the most important forces of this type are summarized in the
following pages.

　　Federal Financial Support. There has been a massive
infusion of funds into the adult higher education system by
the federal government. Educational extension played a role
in almost every piece of social legislation enacted during the
1960s and 1970s—the Higher Education Act, the Elementary
and Secondary Education Act, the Higher Education Facilities Act, the Manpower Development and Training Act, the
Public Health Service Act, the Housing and Urban Development Act, the Foreign Assistance Act, and the Civil Rights
Act. The National Advisory Council on Extension and Continuing Education identified 184 discrete federal programs in
extension, continuing education, and community service
funded at $6.714 billion in 1972, with about $2.35 billion
going directly to institutions of higher education (National
Advisory Council on Extension and Continuing Education,
1972). As a result of these new programs, tremendous de-

mands have been put on universities to provide training for (among others) Vista volunteers, Peace Corps recruits, Job Corps participants, community action leaders, Head Start teachers, paraprofessional workers in rural and innercity projects, employees of government agencies and community problem-solving services, and consultants.

Although many benefits have accrued to higher adult education from this infusion of funds, leaders of the field have expressed conerns about several possible negative consequences: (1) With most federal funds designated for special projects rather than for support of basic continuing programs, there is a tendency toward program fragmentation and diversion from central goals. (2) Many federal projects are of a "crash" nature, with short lead time for planning and unrealistic deadlines; thus, they tend to divert energy from long-run objectives and perpetuate a constant climate of crisis. (3) Status within and among institutions is strongly influenced by a dean's success in obtaining federal grants or contracts; this fosters a spirit of competitiveness among colleagues and a tendency to value "grantsmanship" over broader professional competencies (Knowles, 1969, p. 32).

Equally as significant as the entry of the federal government into supporting adult higher education in the middle 1960s has been the resistance of Congrss to attempts by the Nixon and Ford administrations in the early 1970s to cut back these appropriations. As this period drew to a close, Senator Walter Mondale introduced a bill, the Lifelong Learning Act, to support research and development, teacher training, curriculum development, conversion of facilities to serve adult participants, development of techniques for guidance and counseling of adults, development and dissemination of media materials appropriate for adults, and assessment of the role of gerontology and related field to identify educational needs and goals of elderly Americans. Although Mondale became the vice president and the legislation was enacted, Congress has been reluctant to provide the funds to carry out the purposes.

Demand for Accessibility. Growing pressures from a

variety of sources to make higher education more accessible
to more people—especially part-time working adult students—have produced a rash of nontraditional and external
degree programs. Small experiments in making undergraduate degrees available to adults at their convenience—such as
the Goddard College program started in the 1930s and the
special degrees for adults (Bachelor of Liberal Studies) in
Brooklyn College and the University of Oklahoma in the
1950s—engendered an epidemic of new external degree
programs and other nontraditional study forms in the early
1970s. These programs are presently spreading throughout
the higher education establishment and are starting to bring
about transformations in its mission, structure, program,
educational strategies, clientele, policies, and relationships
with the larger society. Higher education has responded to
the pressure with minimal resistance, and in many cases with
outright enthusiasm, because as the pool of youth available
for college enrollment has declined, finding a new clientele
became a matter of survival.

The Commission on Non-Traditional Study was
formed in 1971 under the auspices of the College Entrance
Examination Board and the Educational Testing Service and
funded by the Carnegie Corporation of New York and the
Educational Foundation of America to investigate nontraditional education programs. The publications of the commission, produced during its two-year lifetime, documented the
need and demand, rationale, revolutionary implications, and
widespread diffusion of nontraditional alternatives for
higher education (Commission on Non-Traditional Study,
1973; Houle, 1973; Gould and Cross, 1972).

Nontraditional programs tend to possess one or more
of the following characteristics: (1) open admissions;
(2) granting of credit for knowledge obtained outside of
academia through a variety of assessment procedures (including the College-Level Examination Program, the College
Proficiency Examination Program, and interviews by panels
or individual mentors); (3) qualification for degrees solely by
examination; (4) utilization of part-time nonfaculty teachers

and mentors; (5) development of individualized learning programs by students with or without the assistance of mentors; (6) fulfillment of learning objectives through contracts; (7) utilization of unconventional methods of learning and teaching (television, audiotapes, videotapes, films, programmed instruction, learning modules, work-study programs, computerized instruction, undirected experience, independent study projects); and (8) inclusion of noneducational institutions (business and industry, community organizations, government agencies) in an educational consortium.

The Continuing Education Unit. A method for quantifying the value of noncredit continuing education activities, the Continuing Education Unit (CEU), has been introduced and widely adopted. The CEU was originally developed by a group of thirty-three national educational, professional, business, and labor associations and government agencies through the Task Force to Study the Feasibility and Implementation of a Uniform Unit for the Measurement of Noncredit Continuing Education Programs. The CEU was approved in 1971 by the Southern Association of Colleges and Schools and spread rapidly across the country. It has since been used widely, especially for advancement and relicensing in the professions.

Concern for Urban Problems. The special problems of urban society have caused urban universities to become more deeply involved in research and educational programs directly concerned with city living and city planning. Many universities have created special administrative units and academic programs (for example, urban affairs centers) to conduct research, offer instruction, and provide services related to urban problems. Others have incorporated these activities into existing operations. Some state universities (notably the University of Wisconsin) employ urban extension agents who serve urban areas in much the same way that agricultural extension agents have served rural areas for over half a century, and bills have been introduced repeatedly into Congress for a national urban extension program.

Increase of Adult Credit Students. The proportion of

older part-time students in credit programs continues to increase steadily. By the fall of 1975, 38.4 percent of all students in postsecondary institutions were enrolled on a part-time basis; 56.1 percent of credit students in community colleges were part time. In 1974, 3.2 million, or one third of the 9.8 million credit students, were twenty-five years old and over; and of these, 1,025,000 were over thirty-five—an increase of 30.2 percent over the previous year. Of the 3.2 million older students, 80 percent were attending on a part-time basis (Postsecondary Education Resources, 1976). In fact, the report of the Committee on the Financing of Higher Education for Adult Students of the American Council on Education in 1974 proposed that it was no longer meaningful to distinguish between "adult" and "regular" students (Postsecondary Education Resources, Inc., 1976). It is clear that as nontraditional and external degree programs continue to make higher education accessible to older working students, adults will continue to constitute an increasing proportion of the clientele of higher education.

Overcoming Geographical Dispersion. New delivery systems for reaching large numbers of people spread over extensive geographic areas have been developed. The Union of Experimenting Colleges and Universities (University Without Walls), headquartered at Antioch University, allows students to work toward undergraduate and graduate degrees without requiring residence on any of the more than thirty campus members of its consortium. The University of Maryland offers full degree programs for military personnel and their dependents on scores of overseas bases of the Department of Defense. Brigham Young University reaches more than a quarter of a million students through a nationwide and worldwide network of centers. Nova University, of Fort Lauderdale, Florida, offers several master's and doctoral degree programs anywhere in the United States where thirty or more students are able to be enrolled in a cluster for regular periodic sessions. Pennsylvania State University, the University of Nebraska, the University of Wisconsin, the California State University and College System, and many other state systems deliver both credit and noncredit programs through networks of university centers, multimedia systems, and consortium arrangements with other state institutions.

Innovative Funding Schemes. New ways of financing higher continuing education are being explored and developed. A major breakthrough occurred in federal support for continuing education when provision was first made for basic opportunity grants to part-time students in the 1975 appropriation for Title IV of the Higher Education Act Amendments of 1972. A number of special task forces and commissions have explored alternatives for state support for continuing higher education—notably in New York, New Jersey, Massachusetts, California, and Iowa. The alternatives considered included: (1) state financing of leadership positions; (2) state financing of information and counseling services; (3) state aid to institutions for adult students; (4) institutional incentive grants; (5) extension of state aid to part-time and noncredit students; (6) an educational entitlement approach, in which individuals are provided with vouchers entitling them to obtain educational services from institutions of their choice; and (7) tax incentives either to individuals or to employers. Recommendations are being presented to several state legislatures regarding one or more of these alternatives.

The Emergence of Consortia. There is a tendency for institutions of higher education to join together into consortia to share resources and operate programs, and often to offer external degrees. These consortia frequently include noneducational organizations—such as corporations, government agencies, and community organizations—as full members. Some consortia are local or metropolitan in scope, such as the Bridgeport (Connecticut) Higher Education Consortium. Others are statewide (for example, the State University of New York and the California State University and College System); regional (for example, the East Central College Consortium and College of Mid-America); or national (for example, the Union of Experimenting Colleges and Universities). The concept of "learning systems" is being super-imposed on the older concept of "educational institutions."

Expansion of Graduate Programs. Graduate programs for training professional adult education workers continue to expand. In 1960, thirteen universities offered master's and doctor's degrees in adult education and produced a few score of graduates; in 1976 some sixty-five universities were grad-uating hundreds of professional adult educators. Indeed, adult education is now one of the few education specialties in which the demand for trained professionals is geater than the supply.

Community Colleges

Until the modern era of adult education, beginning at about the time of World War I, the two-year college was such a peripheral part of the total higher education picture that it was simply incorporated into the statistics of colleges and universities or of secondary education. Even in 1953, only 265,799 students were enrolled in 518 two-year institutions, and these figures had grown to only 852,373 students in 633 institutions by 1963. Between 1963 and 1974, enrollment skyrocketed to 2,919,650 and the number of institutions to 999 (NCES, 1975). A comprehensive survey of the literature of the field in 1962 (Fields, 1962) listed in its bibliography only 19 books on junior and community colleges published between 1927 and 1960. A similar bibliography in 1974 (North Carolina State University, 1974) listed 65 books published since 1960.

No doubt the forces that produced this phenomenal growth in a little over a decade included all of those that produced the ferment in higher education in general. In addition to those forces which were influencing all of higher education, other forces were exerting influences only on the community colleges, causing them to add components to deal with new functions and audiences:

1. An increasing shift from the manufacturing to the service industries produced a larger demand for skilled techni-

cians and paraprofessionals, especially in the allied health fields.

2. Faith in the power of education to open doors to social and economic opportunity caused new entrants into higher education to be more career oriented in their educational goals.

3. The egalitarian spirit of "The Great Society" stimulated federal legislation and aid directed toward the community college as a key institution in bringing about social reform and opportunity for minorities.

4. The shorter commuting distances to most community colleges and their lower tuitions make it possible for working people to engage in higher education through part-time study.

5. The "open door" admission policy of most community colleges rendered past academic difficulties less of a barrier to entry.

6. Competition for admission to four-year colleges has increased, because most community colleges served as "finishing schools" for young women or "prep schools" for young men and women.

As community colleges evolved, they retained this "preparatory" component, typically labeled "the transfer program." A second component, often called "the terminal program," was added to provide career training. A third component, continuing education, grew in the image of university extension but with a more diversified program of noncredit adult education activities. A fourth component, which was still in the early stages of development at the close of this period, was the community service program. Harlacher (1970, pp. 213–214) cites this component as the one that makes the community college a uniquely American institution. "A junior college is an institution that primarily duplicates organizationally and fulfills philosophically the first two years of the four-year senior college. On the other hand, a true community college connotes an institution that has developed beyond an isolated entity into an institution seeking full partnership with its community. In the process, the community college becomes for its district community a cultural center, a focal point of intellectual life, a source of solidarity and a fount of local pride."

Voluntary Organizations

One of the most striking developments of the modern era of adult education has been the rising national awareness of volunteerism as a major national resource. The corps of volunteer workers in the traditional voluntary organizations in the fields of social service, health care, youth agencies, and community service continues to expand; in addition, a rash of new organizations came into being after World War II. Many of the "Great Society" programs of the 1960s—the Peace Corps, the Jobs Corps, Vista (later ACTION), Head Start, Upward Bound, Community Action Projects, and the like— made extensive use of volunteers for educational purposes, many of them drawn from outside the middle-class population traditionally associated with volunteering. But the most explosive growth in volunteerism is in the newly organized endeavors of citizens to cope with social problems or to influence social policy. Some of these new citizen-action movements tend to focus on a single issue, such as civil rights (for example, the Southern Christian Leadership Conference), environmental protection (the Sierra Club, CONCERN), the Vietnam War (the Vietnam Moratorium), feminism (NOW), or abortion (Right to Life). Others, such as John Gardner's Common Cause, serve as vehicles for attacking a multitude of problems confronting the citizenry, including housing, consumer protection, waste disposal, transportation, taxes, crime, pollution, governmental efficiency, and the like. Some of these organizations operate only at the national level; others attack local and state problems as well as national problems through local and state chapters.

New organizations have been created to coordinate the programs of individual action groups and systematize their efforts. Examples in the field of "organized" volunteerism include the Association for Administration of

Volunteer Services, the Association of Volunteer Bureaus, the Corporate Volunteer Coordinators Council, and the National Society of Directors of Volunteer Services. Examples of organizations serving the newly organized and grassroots voluntary movements are the National Center for a Voluntary Society, the National Center for Voluntary Action, and the Alliance for Volunteerism. A vehicle for stimulating, assembling, and disseminating scholarly research on volunteerism was established with the founding in 1971 of the Association of Voluntary Action Scholars and the beginning of the publication of its quarterly *Journal of Voluntary Action Research*.

Finally, a major development in voluntary organizations, particularly during the 1970s, has been the widespread growth of continuing professional education. Spurred on partly by the passage in a number of states of laws requiring periodic relicensing, professional associations of nurses, physicians, lawyers, dentists, engineers, teachers, and other service providers have launched continuing education programs, often in collaboration with university professional schools.

Educational Brokering

The concept of educational brokering has roots that go back to the early years of the adult education movement. Many libraries began to maintain card files of community resources to which clients could be referred. Since 1923, the Educational Exchange of Greater Boston (formerly the Prospect Union Educational Exchange) has been providing adult education information and counseling. Several local adult education councils, notably in Cleveland, Denver, and New York, provide similar services. But with the rapid growth of adult education in the 1970s, educational brokering is an idea whose time had come again.

Educational brokering has been described as "an intermediary function, a mechanism by which adults may take advantage of the broad array of learning opportunities in their communities. Brokers aid individuals through advisement, assessment, and advocacy as they move into the often strange territory of postsecondary education. Brokers help people make personal and career decisions, select appropriate educational resources, and embark on learning programs. The distinctiveness of brokering arises from (1) the ways clients are reached and served in their own communities, usually utilizing existing resources, and (2) perhaps most important, the new educational role of client advocate. The interests of individuals, not institutions, is the focus of brokers' advocacy efforts" (Center for Educational Brokering, 1976, p. 1).

Brokerage agencies now flourish all over the country under a variety of names, including the Center for Adult Learning in Boulder, Colorado; the Career Counseling Service in Providence, Rhode Island; the Educational Opportunity Center Program in Boston; the Regional Learning Service of Central New York in Syracuse; the Center for Open Learning in Demopolis, Alabama; Community-Based Counseling for Adults in Madison, Wisconsin; the Rockland County Guidance Center for Women in Nyack, New York; and the Learning Exchange in Evanston, Illinois. There appear to be four patterns of organization among the new centers: (1) free-standing agencies, which are attached to no other institution and are supported by combinations of client fees, state and federal funds, and contracts with corporations; (2) new units in existing systems (such as the Hudson Community College Commission in Jersey City), in which governing structures are linked to the broader system and funding comes mainly from that system; (3) consortium centers, in which a headquarters staff coordinates a network of counselor-advocates situated in the individual colleges of the consortium who advise clients of learning opportunities throughout the network; and (4) new units within established institutions (such as the School for New Learning at DePaul University) which are funded and administered by a single institution yet refer clients to a variety of institutions.

Many of the brokering agencies gained their initial support from the Fund for the Improvement of Postsecondary Education and the National Institute for Education. But between 1974 and 1976, support for local and state brokering agencies was built into legislation in California, Massachusetts, New Jersey, and Pennsylvania. On January 1, 1976, the national Center for Educational Brokering was established to promote educational brokering through technical assistance, publications, and public policy studies and recommendations. It publishes a monthly bulletin describing new developments.

The Dynamics of Adult Education

The most visible characteristic of the system of adult education is its expansiveness and flexibility. As has been documented earlier in this chapter, adult education has a history of adapting to new social needs and serving elements of the population previously unreached; it has spread to an ever-wider spectrum of institutions; it has developed new techniques and media; and it recruits and trains large numbers of new personnel to deliver its services. Enrollment figures in almost every institutional setting show dramatic increases. A survey by the Response Analysis Corporation of Princeton, New Jersey, in 1972 showed that 32.1 million adults (more than one out of every three) were engaged in systematic learning that year and that 47.7 million additional "would-be learners" desired to participate in some form of adult educational activity (Cross, Valley, and Associates, 1974).

Clearly, the adult education function of most institutions is moving from the peripheral status it occupied for so long toward a more central status. Indeed, institutions of higher education are moving away from being almost exclusively youth-serving organizations to becoming predominately adult-serving organizations. Meanwhile, the system is demonstrating a high degree of creativity in its ability to invent new institutional forms—residential centers, external degree programs, clearinghouses, brokering agencies, and the like—to meet new needs.

Several current trends seem to augur a period of

major change in the whole educational system in the near future. The most potent of these is lifelong education, based on the notion that in a world of accelerating change, learning must be a continuing process from birth to death, and that therefore society must provide educational resources and services throughout the life-span. A related trend is that toward self-directed learning, based on the notion that it is no longer sufficient for individuals to be taught what others already know, but they must acquire the skills of self-directed inquiry so that they can discover new knowledge continuously. A third trend is toward the unity of education, work, and life, based on the notion that learning is most effective when it is related to and integrated with working and living. When combined, these three trends predict a new kind of educational system that would bring all the institutions of society into a consortium to provide continuous or recurrent learning experiences for self-directed inquirers throughout their life-span. The days of separate institutions for elementary, secondary, higher, and adult education seem to be numbered.

Chapter Three

Typology of Adult Learning Systems

Wayne L. Schroeder

Finding order in the field of adult education is not an easy task. The dynamic system reflects kaleidoscopic variety in agent and client actions. Yet, an underlying order can be discerned by focusing on the fundamental processes of program planning. From this perspective, agent, client, and program relationships can be explored in terms of propositions for research.

This chapter is essentially a search for order in adult education. More specifically, its purpose is to analyze agent systems, client systems, and the program development process. The typology that results is intended to help practitioners become more discriminating in their use of knowledge and researchers more realistic and generative in their search for knowledge.

As the chapter unfolds, it will become apparent that a particular perspective of the field is being reflected: Adult education is viewed as a developmental process used to link various agent and adult client systems for the purpose of establishing directions and procedures for adult learning programs. Accordingly, initial effort will be focused on classifying and explicating various agent systems that serve adult education functions followed by an effort to type and explicate various adult client systems. Then the developmental process itself will be examined as it unfolds into major program decisions of a directional and procedural nature. Next, a system for discerning control-orientation decision patterns will be presented. Finally, the resultant control-orientation patterns will be reduced to form three major program types—agent oriented, client oriented, and eclectic.

Agent Systems

Two categories of agent systems may be stipulated on the basis of the primary roles they perform—leadership systems and operating systems. The primary role of leadership systems is to furnish guidance and direction to the field by establishing broad goals and policies, allocating resources, training leaders, and generating knowledge. In contrast, the primary role of operating systems is to plan and conduct adult education programs for various adult clienteles. It should be recognized, however, that agencies of each category do perform roles of the other, although the adopted role remains subordinate and instrumental to the agency's primary role. Whereas adult education programs of leadership agencies are generally aimed at implementation of broad goals and guidelines, leadership efforts of operating agencies are generally aimed at altering those goals, guidelines, or laws that affect the scope and effectiveness of their particular operation.

Leadership Systems

There are four types of leadership systems in adult education: (1) state, regional, and national governments; (2)

professional associations of adult education; (3) private
foundations; and (4) graduate programs of adult education. Though related by role, each type performs special
functions.

State, Regional, and National Governments. Systems of
this type furnish direction to the field through funding policies, information dissemination, and coordination. An obvious example is the federal government, whose involvement
in adult education is extensive. An estimated $50 to $60 billion of the U.S. gross national product goes into adult education each year. In 1971, there were 143 federally supported
adult education programs in the U.S. that addressed such
diverse areas as educational personnel development, public
health, vocational education, miscellaneous education for
the general public, agricultural production and rural life,
veterans' education, and community problems. These programs were established by over 100 discrete laws, and nearly
every major federal department and agency was responsible
for one or more of them.

In spite of its massive involvement in adult education,
the federal government has generally maintained a facilitating rather than a controlling posture. Two principles guide
its practice: "The first of these is that government should
have no role in providing resources and affecting social systems if these can be achieved with reasonable effectiveness by
nongovernmental units. The second is consistent with this,
namely, that nothing should be carried out by a higher, more
centralized unit of government that can be effectively
achieved by a lesser unit of government" (Delker, 1974, p.
28). Beyond these two principles there is no explicit overall
federal policy for adult education, but there are some central
tendencies in its activities that imply policy. First, although
general federal support for adult education has never been
adopted, support continues in the form of specific legislation
aimed at particular clienteles or particular areas of need or
both. Second, procedures reflect and encourage local and
state autonomy in determining priorities. Accordingly, there
has been a trend away from funding a few established educational institutions and toward funding a variety of agencies,

including voluntary associations, community action agencies, and private businesses. Third, emphasis in this country is being placed on coordination of activities, as exemplified by establishment of the National Advisory Council on Extension and Continuing Education in 1965 and by the president's appointment of a National Advisory Council on Adult Education in 1970. The final trend in federal activity concerns clientele priority: Since the early 1960s, a broad band of legislation has been enacted to aid the disadvantaged segments of society through educative means.

In addition to the extensive leadership activity of the federal government, regional and state governments have also been active in establishing policy, monitoring programs, allocating monies, coordinating activities, and training leaders. Every state department of education now employs at least one individual responsible for adult education. In addition, a number of states have established representative committees to help plan and coordinate activities of various organizations in their states.

Professional Associations of Adult Education. Professional associations in general are classified as operating systems rather than leadership systems. Professional associations of adult education, however, because of the leadership they exert in the field, are also classified as leadership systems. Houle (cited in Griffith, 1970) has developed a typology for associations of adult education based on the focus of membership interest and commitment. Houle identified the following five subtypes:

1. Content: Members have a commitment to a particular message they wish to deliver to all adults. Included are religious adult educators, adult educators working for world peace, and adult educators in the family planning area.

2. Sponsorship agency: Members are committed to and work within a specific institutional agency that conducts adult education. Examples are the Association for Continuing Higher Education; the National Association for Public Continuing and Adult Education; the National University Extension Association; and the National Community Education Association.

3. Method: Members are identified with a particular method. Examples include the National Home Study Council, the Residential Adult Education Section of the Adult Education Association of the U.S.A., and the National Association of Educational Broadcasters.

4. Place: Members are organized on the basis of geographic location. Examples are the Northern Illinois Round Table of Adult Educators, the Adult Education Association of the U.S.A., the Canadian Association for Adult Education, and various community and state adult education planning and coordinating councils.

5. Clientele: Members identify themselves with a particular adult clientele. Examples include labor union educators, correctional educators, and business and industry educators.

Private Foundations. Like federal and state governments, private foundations influence the field through their selective funding policies and procedures. Three foundations—Carnegie, Kellogg, and Ford—have been most prominent in adult education. The Carnegie Foundation has been primarily concerned with exchange of information and knowledge, advancement of theory and practice, and public acceptance of adult education. The W. K. Kellogg Foundation has been associated primarily with the establishment of residential centers for continuing education in the United States and abroad. The Ford Foundation has exerted its greatest influence through establishment of the Fund for Adult Education, which financed the formation of the Center for the Study of Liberal Education for Adults, a cornerstone in the development of a literature base of the field.

Graduate Programs of Adult Education. Leadership exercised by graduate programs is a form quite different from that exercised by other leadership systems. Their influence is manifested primarily in the leaders they prepare and in the knowledge they produce. A U.S. survey conducted in 1970–71 revealed that nine universities were awarding degrees at the bachelor's level, 59 at the master's level, and 38 at the doctoral level (Griffith and Cloutier, 1974). By 1971, these same institutions had graduated a total of 4,453 people, one fourth of whom had earned doctorates. In addition, through the years professors employed in graduate programs have conducted countless nondegree workshops, institutes, and short courses designed to prepare and upgrade teachers, program planners, and administrators. Equal in importance have been the contributions of professors and students alike in formulating the discipline of adult education. This process has been accomplished by systematically borrowing concepts and research findings from related disciplines, such as sociology, psychology, and gerontology, and increasingly by generating concepts and research findings from direct observation of the field itself.

Operating Systems

There are three types of operating systems in adult education: (1) institutional agencies; (2) voluntary associations; and (3) individual agents. Unlike leadership systems, whose activities furnish global guidance and direction and whose influence generally spans geographic communities, operating systems are primarily concerned with planning and conducting educative programs for client systems that are often in the same geographic community as the operating system itself. The three basic types may be identified from an examination of the general nature of the parent organization within which adult education functions. Each of the types is further subclassified according to the primary purpose of the parent unit and the degree to which adult education has penetrated its structure.

Institutional Agencies. An institutional agency is "an organized group carrying out a particular institutional function. For example, a specific religious denomination would be an institutional agency of the religious institution" (Theodorson and Theodorson, 1969, p. 207). These agencies operate within traditional and often legally mandated purposes and allocation of resources. The flow of authority is hierarchical, being ultimately derived from the general public through stockholders of self-perpetuated boards

(Houle, 1972). Institutional agencies are formal groups, as are voluntary associations. The important difference is that institutional agencies have employees who perform specified leadership roles. The following four subtypes of institutional agencies may be stipulated on the basis of their major purposes and the degree to which adult education processes have been incorporated into their structures and routines (Schroeder, 1970).

1. Autonomous adult education agencies: This subgroup includes agencies whose primary purpose is to address systematically the general or specific learning needs and interests of adult clienteles. Adult education is a central and imperative part of their structure, and they include proprietary schools, consulting firms, and both residential and nonresidential adult education centers that have developed independently of the regular school system. They may be either profit or nonprofit, and they generally fall under the control of either boards of directors or trustees. Autonomy is an important quality of their character.

2. Youth education agencies: These are agencies whose primary purpose is to address systematically the preparatory learning needs of youth; adult education is a secondary component of their structure, and they include elementary and secondary schools, vocational-technical schools, community colleges, and four-year colleges and universities. Adult education subsystems of these agencies assume a variety of labels more or less reflective of function or normative pattern. Elementary and secondary schools house what are called adult evening or day programs, adult learning centers, adult high schools, or even community schools. Community colleges frequently refer to their adult education units as "community service divisions" or "continuing education divisions." Similarly, four-year colleges have largely adopted the continuing education label to refer to their form of adult education. Universities operate what are variously called general extension divisions, continuing education offices, nontraditional degree programs, evening colleges, and both residential and nonresidential centers. Addi-

tionally, land grant universities house the extensive adult education operation known as the Cooperative Extension Service.

Two additional descriptive features of youth education agencies should be noted. First, in the case of private organizations, control is usually in the hands of a board of directors or trustees. In the case of public schools, control is embodied in governmental departments and lay boards; authority, however, ultimately rests with the general public. Public youth education agencies are manifestations of the institutionalization of the value of education. Second, although all agencies of this type have adopted adult education as a secondary component, the degree to which that component has been functionally integrated into the parent structure varies. For example, adult education in elementary and secondary schools as well as vocational-technical schools tends generally to be more integrated into the parent structure than does adult education in colleges and universities. Continuing education and extension divisions of universities, for example, may and often do exercise considerable functional autonomy.

3. Community service agencies: The primary purpose of agencies in this category is to serve the collective and individual needs of a community or some segment thereof; adult education is an allied component of their structure. Examples are libraries, museums, health agencies, welfare agencies, social work agencies, family counseling agencies, law enforcement agencies, correctional agencies, and recreational centers. Though it is customary to consider these agencies public, or at least nonprofit, they may also be private profit-making organizations. They are distinct from autonomous adult education agencies and youth education agencies in that their primary reason for being is not education. Rather, their mandate is to render service to individuals and groups in need. Adult education, then, assumes an allied position along with noneducative means of rendering that service. For example, a correctional agency has adopted adult education as an allied component of its structure when it (a) recognizes

that to isolate a group of adult offenders is merely a temporary means of protecting society and (b) launches a parallel educative campaign to prevent crime and resocialize offenders.

An important distinction can be made within the common characteristics of community service agencies: Libraries and museums are primarily in the business of storing and retrieving general and specialized information in such forms as books, exhibits, and films. In contrast, other community service agencies mentioned are concerned with preventing or remediating particular social problems or needs.

4. Special interest agencies: Agencies whose primary purpose is to serve special interests are included in this category; adult education is a subordinate component of their structure. Business and industrial corporations are examples of special interest agencies. Religious groups and the armed forces are less obvious examples. All four agencies have special interests to pursue, and in each case, adult education is viewed as instrumental yet distinctly subordinate to their special interests. The nature of interest varies, however, as does its breadth of interpretation. Businesses and industries appear to be relatively narrow in the educative interpretation of their interest, tending to become involved only in adult education that leads directly to profit. In contrast, many religious groups and the armed forces are rather broad in the interpretation of their interests. Some religious groups have so secularized their activities that they function as much as community service agencies as special interest agencies. Similarly, many nonduty educational programs of the armed forces appear to interpret very broadly the military's special interest in protecting the country from internal and external armed threats. For instance, the Defense Action for Nontraditional Educational Services (DANTES) seems to be as broad and socially preparatory a by-function as many of the adult education programs of youth education agencies.

Unlike the other three agencies (autonomous, youth education, and community service agencies), special interest agencies direct their programs primarily toward their employees or members. There are, of course, exceptions: Businesses often conduct educational programs for adult customers, and religious agencies frequently extend education service to adults who are not members.

Voluntary Associations. A voluntary association is defined by Lumberg, Schrag, and Larsen (1963, p. 119) as "a relatively lasting collectivity, somewhat formally organized, whose members belong by their own choice." They are satellites rather than operational extensions of our basic institutions. They tend to be more adaptive than institutional agencies. They can and often do arise quickly in response to special interest needs and problems, either as a means of satisfying them or of advocating that other agencies satisfy them. In contrast to institutional agencies, control in voluntary associations rests largely with members rather than with governing boards. Workers, especially at the local level, are usually unpaid volunteers rather than paid employees. Purposes tend to reflect immediate, specific special interests and concerns compared with the long-range, broad, often mandated concerns reflected in the purposes of institutional agencies. As a consequence of some of these differences, adult education activities of voluntary associations tend to be more atomistic and ad hoc than those of institutional agencies. Like institutional agencies, however, their adult education substructures tend to assume a form and function consistent with the purposes and normative patterns of the parent organization.

Bloomberg (1969) identified four types of voluntary associations according to their primary purpose. These four types may, with some adaptation, also be used to subtype voluntary associations as a major type of operating system in adult education, because adult education tends to be used by an organization to achieve its purposes.

1. Pressure groups: These are associations whose primary purpose is to secure some advantage for their members; adult education is used to make member and non-member groups aware of their purpose and to make members able to perform various political roles. Examples include farmers' organizations, unions, and veterans' organizations.

Their purpose is most closely associated with special interest agencies.

2. Community betterment organizations and service clubs: Associations whose primary purpose is to render some service to the community or to some segment of it are included. Adult education is used to focus public attention on particular problems or issues and to develop a membership capability to plan and implement relevant forms of action. Examples are ad hoc community planning and action groups, the League of Women Voters, the Rotary Club, the Kiwanis Club, the Lions Club, and chambers of commerce. Their function is quite similar to community service agencies.

3. Mutual benefit societies and social clubs: Associations whose primary purpose is to confer status and promote an elite fellowship are placed in this category. Adult education is used to socialize members into the traditions and rituals of the association and, in some cases, to facilitate the pursuit of learning interests of members. Primary examples are the orders of Moose, Elks, Eagles, and Odd Fellows.

4. Professional associations: These are associations whose primary purpose is to advance knowledge and improve practice in various specialized areas; adult education is used to enhance public image and update member knowledge and capability. Examples are the Adult Education Association of the U.S.A., the American Academy of Orthopedic Surgeons, the Association for Continuing Higher Education, and the American Bar Association. Their central concern with adult education and their autonomy make them most like autonomous adult education agencies.

Individual Agents. The final category of operating systems is individual agents. In a sense, the adult education agent is always an individual. The individual agent of this category, however, represents him- or herself rather than an agency or association. The structural elements with which the agent contends are individual in nature rather than organizational. Instead of being tied to organizational missions, roles, and role expectations, the individual agent may express personal goals, capabilities, and interests. Two basic types of individual agents may be stipulated on the basis of their primary purpose and the use to which they put the processes of adult education:

1. The entrepreneur is an individual whose explicit intent is to profit by systematically conveying his expertise to others. The agent may be called a tutor or a consultant; the former conveys a rather tightly arranged system of knowledge or skill to another individual, and the latter uses process and content skills to help individuals and groups solve problems. With respect to autonomy and risk, the individual entrepreneur as an agent system operates similarly to autonomous adult education agencies.

2. The volunteer is an individual whose intent is the systematic sharing of expertise with others for reasons of personal satisfaction, service, or both. Volunteers are often retired or otherwise independent and have free time. They may function similarly to the entrepreneurial tutor or consultant or similarly to a volunteer working within an institutional agency or a voluntary association. The individual volunteer, however, is normally able to exercise maximum freedom in negotiating educational activities with his or her adult learners.

Client Systems

Client systems of adult education are many and varied. At the most general level, they may be classified as either membership or nonmembership systems. In membership systems, the agent relates to learners as members of a formal group or organization. In nonmembership systems, the agent relates to learners on some basis other than their membership in formal groups. For the sake of convenience, nonmembership systems are sometimes referred to as nominal, ad hoc, or designated groups. It is important to recognize, however, that they are not groups in the formal sense. A formal group is "a social group whose structure and activities have been rationally organized and standardized with definitely prescribed group goals, rules, and leaders" (Theodorson and Theodorson, 1969, p. 177).

Membership Client Systems

As indicated above, agents relate to membership client systems with explicit recognition that learners involved are members of the system. Furthermore, through prescription or through the process of socialization, group goals and norms often become individual goals and standards and are used as a basis for assessing educational needs and for planning educational programs. The two basic types of membership client systems are internal agent membership and external agent membership.

Internal Agent Membership Systems. In these systems, learners are integral parts of the agent structure itself. They may hold staff or leadership positions in the organization or may just be members. Any agent system that plans or delivers educational programs for its members is using an internal agent membership client system. Programs that serve employed members of an organization are usually referred to as staff development or training programs and are common among the leadership systems and institutional agency systems discussed earlier in this chapter. Programs that serve members who assume elected or volunteer leadership positions within an organization are generally referred to as leadership training programs and are commonly found in voluntary associations, as are programs designed for the general membership. The best examples of general membership programs are those within annual conferences of professional associations.

External Agent Membership Systems. These systems are similar to the internal agent membership type, except clients are not integral parts of the agent system itself but are members of another organization with which the agent system is interacting. Any organization that interacts with another to the end that an adult education program is planned or conducted for members of the latter is using an external agent membership system. Program labels used are the same as those used for internal agent membership systems. Depending on the nature and level of members targeted, programs may be called staff development, employee training, leadership development, or general membership development. Examples abound among both leadership and operating agencies. At the operating level, professors of adult education conduct workshops and institutes for faculty and staff of various institutional agencies; the United States Office of Education initiates a system of residential workshops for state leaders of adult education. At the operating level, colleges and universities jointly plan and conduct staff development and training programs to orient or upgrade employees or members of professional associations, unions, business firms, law enforcement offices, and the Armed Forces. The Cooperative Extension Service is involved in planning and delivering educational programs for employees of farm commodity organizations and agri-business. And libraries furnish planning and materials services to employees of school systems and to members of numerous community organizations.

Nonmembership Client Systems

As indicated earlier, learners in nonmember client systems are not organized on the basis of membership in a formal group but on the basis of some other criterion, such as geography, demographic characteristics, social roles, interests, or individual or social need. Use of the first three criteria is based on the assumption that the criteria themselves are correlated with educational needs and interests. In contrast, social roles and interests are direct expressions of educational interests and needs.

Geographic Criteria. Groups located in neighborhood, district, community, or supra-community areas are included here. For example, a district program would be a community service designed for residents of a community college district. Community client systems are targeted by various community development and service efforts of single agent systems or by a complex of agent systems working together. Still other programs that consider the general community as their client systems are mass media programs sponsored by various institutional agencies; educational exhibits presented by museums; public affairs lecture series and discussion groups sponsored by public libraries; and community service programs sponsored by religious organizations. The final type of geographic system, supra-community, is exemplified by regional, national, and international development programs.

Demographic Criteria. Age, sex, race, education, and income are characteristics commonly used to designate nonmember client systems. For example, numerous agent systems are found operating adult education programs for the aged, women, racial groups, the undereducated, and the poor. Since the early 1960s, a great deal of emphasis has been placed on the latter two client systems, and a plethora of legislative enactments have encouraged institutional programs for them.

Social Role Criteria. These are used by most adult educators as a basis of designating client systems. Roles that constitute the focus of many programs include those of citizen, parent, worker, and student. Thus, there are programs dealing with public affairs, home and family, occupations, and nontraditional degree programs for adults.

Interest Criteria. These may to some extent move people to participate in any or all programs previously mentioned. Some programs, however, are designed especially to appeal to the more individualistic and expressive human impulses rather than basic physical or social needs. Leisure and cultural programs reflect concern for a client system based on interests. The content of these programs varies but is always avocational in nature and self-fulfilling in effect.

Individual and Social Need Systems. Special physical, psychological, or social needs of individuals are included here. As may be expected, these systems overlap somewhat with those based on demographics and social roles. However, emphasis here is placed on people who have individual or socially debilitating needs and problems. Community service agencies and certain voluntary associations make extensive use of the individual and social need criterion as a basis for designating their client systems. Such broad areas of emphasis include programs for the economically dependent, the

physically and mentally handicapped, and the socially malad-
justed.

The Adult Education Development Process

Adult education is being viewed in this chapter as a
developmental process that links various agent and adult client systems together for the purpose of establishing directions and procedures for programs of adult learning. Having
defined and described agent and client system types, we turn
now to the third major component: the adult education development process.

The adult education development process involves six
major decision points, each of which receives input from variables inherent in the agent and client systems involved.
These variables interact with decision points to form a developmental system (see Figure 1). The decisions have to do
with what will be done and how it will be done. They are of
two levels, macro and micro. Macro decisions establish gen-

Figure 1. The Developmental System

Agent Inputs	Decision Points	Client Inputs
← ——————→	Macro level ←	——————————→
Values		Values
Goals	Educative needs	Goals
Resource capabilities and dispositions	Program objectives	Resource capabilities and dispositions
	Program procedures	
← ——————→	Micro level ←	——————————→
Performance standards	Learning needs	Performance standards
	Learning objectives	
Agent capabilities and dispositions	Learning experiences	Learner capabilities and dispositions

eral directions and program procedures. Micro decisions are more specific and are commonly called instructional or learning decisions.

Decisions vary with the nature and source of inputs that are allowed to influence them. The sections that follow define and explicate the decision points and variables of the system illustrated in Figure 1. Subsequent sections will show that the influences affecting decisions are a function of established control and orientation patterns, which may be used as a basis for formulating three program types—agent centered, client centered, and eclectic.

Macro Decision Points

Macro decision points deal with determining educative need, program objectives, and program procedures. Educative need is essentially a gap in capability which obstructs the successful pursuit of agent or client goals and values. Program objectives are general directional statements that record the educational need to be addressed and the clients to be targeted. Program procedure decisions deal with how the program structure will be designed and how its operation will be supported or facilitated. Structure, in this sense, is synonymous with what Verner and Booth (1964, p. 68) call method: "A method establishes a relationship between the learner and the institution or agency through which the educational task is accomplished." Support decisions are concerned with financial and physical resources (requiring resource acquisition), skilled leadership (requiring leadership selection and training), psychological ownership by client and agent systems (requiring client recruitment and participation), acceptance by those in positions of power (requiring cooptation and coordination), and subsequent knowledge of results (requiring evaluation). The significance of these factors and the corresponding functions depends on the nature of resource capability and the relative inputs of agent and client systems concerned.

Micro Decision Points

Micro decision points concern learning needs, learning objectives, and learning experiences. Learning needs are specific cognitive, affective, and psychomotor "gaps" (Bloom, 1964), which are presumed to constitute important obstacles to developing capabilities and are made explicit in the program objective. Gagne and Briggs (1974) suggest that learning needs refer to behaviors in the categories of verbal information, intellectual skills, cognitive strategies, motor skills, and attitudes. Learning objectives are specific directional statements that record both learner performances and the criteria and conditions upon which performances are measured (Mager, 1975). Finally, learning experience decisions deal with how the "learning structure" will be established and how it will be maintained or facilitated. As used here, learning structure is essentially synonomous with what Verner and Booth (1964, p. 75) call techniques and devices. "The techniques of adult education identify the way in which the instructional agent establishes a relationship between the learner and the learning tasks." *Device* is defined as, "a convenient way of identifying the many instructional aids that extend or increase the effectiveness of methods and techniques but which cannot themselves instruct" (Verner and Booth, 1964, p. 84). Learning maintenance and facilitation, as the second category of learning experience decisions, transcends structure and is concerned with establishing and maintaining an interpersonal climate conducive to learning and growth. According to Knowles (1970, p. 60), there are four basic characteristics of an educational environment that make it conducive to learning: "(1) respect for personality; (2) participation in decision making; (3) freedom of expression and availability of information; and (4) mutual responsibility in defining goals, planning and conducting activities and evaluation."

Macro Input Variables

Macro input variables include values, goals, and resource capabilities and dispositions of agent and client systems. Values, in the sense used here, are predispositions to work toward certain ends with the use of certain means. Thus values are of primary significance, for they affect the other two macro variables, goals and resource capabilities and dispositions. At the most general level, there appear to be four basic values to which agents and clients alike may be committed: (1) individual growth and potential; (2) social well-being; (3) spiritual well-being; and (4) system control and maintenance. These values are reflected both in the goals of operating agencies reported in the 1970 *Handbook of Adult Education* (Smith, Aker, and Kidd, 1970) and in the goals of clients who engage in adult education as revealed in a 1972 national participation study (Cross, Valley, and Associates, 1974). As examples, some of the agency and client goals found in these two documents are catalogued below under the basic values they appear to reflect:

I. Individual growth and potential
    A. Agency goals
        1. Museum: to help individuals interpret objects of their interest
        2. Community college: to develop skills for the effective use of leisure time
        3. Library: to satisfy the topical interests of individuals and groups in the community
        4. Cooperative Extension Service: to help people develop capability to identify and solve directly the problems affecting their lives
    B. Client reasons
        1. To become better informed
        2. To become happier
        3. To get away from routine
II. Social well-being
    A. Agency goals
        1. Health and welfare agencies: to improve the general state of health and welfare of citizens
        2. Community college: to help communities solve problems and conduct long-range planning

3. University: to help solve social and technical problems
4. Library: to serve information needs of disadvantaged, handicapped, home-bound, and institutionalized groups
5. Community development agencies: to enhance the effectiveness with which community resources are used to solve problems plaguing the community

B. Client reasons
1. To meet new people
2. To understand community problems
3. To become a better parent
4. To become a better citizen

III. Spiritual well-being
A. Agency goals
1. Protestant church: to help people search for a link between the divine and the secular
2. Jewish synagogue: to reaffirm a definition of Jewish identity within the larger culture
3. Catholic church: to disseminate Catholic truths and useful knowledge and promote the moral and intellectual culture of its members

B. Client reasons
1. To serve the church
2. To secure a feeling of spiritual well-being
3. To develop a sense of belongingness

IV. System maintenance and control
A. Agency goals
1. Correctional agencies: to rehabilitate offenders
2. University and college: to develop leadership for all levels of community
3. Public school: to provide citizens with a basic elementary and secondary education and to effect responsible citizenry
4. Community college: to help people develop employable skills
5. Labor union: to make members more effective unionists

    6. Business and industry: to increase profit through enhancing job performance

    7. Voluntary associations: to satisfy the interests of members and to improve the performance of leaders

B. Client reasons

    1. To become a better citizen

    2. To satisfy certification requirements

The last macro input variables to be considered are the resource capability and disposition variables (see Figure 1). These variables tend to have greatest impact on procedural decisions and, like goals, are to some extent a reflection of basic values of the agent and client systems concerned. At the most general level is a variable that may be called commitment to a general mode of operation. Agents and clients alike tend to lean either toward education or toward action as general modes of operation. Those committed to education are inclined to value it as an end in itself, while those committed to action value education only as a means to some tangible result or activity. Agents with educational dispositions tend to state objectives in terms of solving specific problems—human or organizational. Clients with educational dispositions tend to value learning for its own sake and participate in a great variety of learning experiences. In contrast, clients with action dispositions tend to limit their learning to that which is applicable to action-oriented goals. Houle calls the former class of clients "learning oriented" and the latter class "goal oriented" (Houle, 1961).

In addition to capabilities and dispositions with respect to a general mode of operation, five other, more specific variables affect procedural decisions.

    1. *Agent-to-Client and Client-to-Agent Linkage Dispositions.* Examples are: (a) a business firm's concern for employees versus a community college's concern for the entire community; (b) clients who have a distinct preference for the entire community; (c) clients who have a distinct preference for the university or college versus clients who do not care where they learn as long as they learn what they want.

2. *Method Capability and Disposition.* Examples are: (a) a private correspondence school that uses a variety of individual, group, and community methods; (b) clients who feel they learn best through individual methods versus clients who feel able to engage in any method as long as it is available and appropriate for their objectives.

3. *Spatial Capability and Disposition.* Examples are: (a) a residential center that requires travel to a single location versus a public school that extends its services to a variety of neighborhood centers throughout the community; (b) client systems that are concentrated in one physical space close to the agent system (as in the case of military personnel on a base) versus client systems that are widely dispersed and removed from the agent system (as in the case of teachers scattered across a state whose in-service training needs are being satisfied by a single university).

4. *Content Capability and Disposition.* Examples are: (a) an evening college part-time degree program that restricts its concern to the transmission of a prescribed body of knowledge associated with the degree in question versus a community development agency that concerns itself with any or all knowledge relevant to the resolution of a community problem it has identified as important; (b) clients without the prerequisite interest and capability to profit from an occupational skill development program offered by a vocational-technical school versus clients that possess such prerequisite interest and capability.

5. *Financial Capability and Disposition.* Examples are: (a) a proprietary school that depends exclusively on client tuition to support its operation versus a continuing education center that receives financial support from the state line budget, private and government grants, and client tuition; (b) clients who are not able to pay for their education versus clients who are able to pay for their education.

From examples given above, it should be apparent that values, goals, and resource capabilities and dispositions of an agent may not always fit those of a client. The desired state obviously is a reasonably good fit (Peters and Boshier,

1976). Under conditions of free choice and spontaneity, there is a natural tendency toward compatability. Where linkage between agent and client is in response to some social or organizational requirement, however, compatibility may not occur. In the latter case, exercise of some power by the agent system or by the client system is frequently necessary to secure compliance (Etzioni, 1961).

Micro Input Variables

Micro input variables include performance standards and the capabilities and dispositions of both agent and client systems (Figure 1). Performance standards affect learning need and learning objective decision points. More specifically, they constitute half of the formula used to compute need: Need is computed by subtracting current levels of cognitive, affective, and psychomotor performance from desired levels of performance. Performance standards of agent and client systems set the desired levels.

Capabilities and dispositions comprise the second major class of micro input variables. Collectively they affect learning experience decisions. Variables of primary concern are those dealing with style, technique, and professionalism.

Agents have leadership styles and clients have learning styles. Leadership style operates on a transactive-interactive continuum. Similarly, learning style operates on a passive-active continuum. At the risk of oversimplification, an example is that transactive leaders encourage one-way communications and therefore tend to be compatible with passive learners; whereas interactive leaders tend to be compatible with active learners.

With respect to technique, an agent may be bound by capability or disposition to a specific instructional technique or may be free to choose from an array of techniques the one that best fits the learners' capabilities and dispositions and the nature of the learning objectives. Similarly, the client may be bound by capability or disposition to a particular technique or possess the capabilities and dispositions that allow freedom of choice. As was the case with performance standards, some agreement between agent and client technique capability and disposition is crucial. One can imagine the difficulty that would arise in a situation where an agent imposes discussion on a group of antisocial clients who lack skill in performing participant discussion roles.

Finally, the professional level of the leader may be an important factor in the learning experience. Its importance depends on particular dispositions of the client system concerned. For example, a highly educated, status-conscious group of clients may resist use of a volunteer as an educational leader. Conversely, a group of undereducated clients who have acquired fear and mistrust of school and professional people may be very receptive to a volunteer leader, particularly one indigenous to the group itself.

Patterns of Decision, Control, and Orientation

In the previous sections it was suggested that agent and client input of various kinds and intensity dynamically interact within crucial program decision points to form a developmental system. We will now examine that dynamic interaction more closely in an effort to discern patterns of decision control and orientation. More specifically, the intent is to formulate patterns that reflect both source and volume of inputs that feed four major developmental decisions. These four developmental decisions relate to the six decision points in Figure 1 in the following way: the determinations of educative need and program objectives are together considered directional in nature, and therefore are labeled "Macro Directions" (I.A in Figure 2). Program procedures in Figure 1 are "Macro Procedures" (I.B in Figure 2). Similarly, the determinations of learning needs and objectives are "Micro Directions" (II.A), and the development of learning experiences is "Micro Procedures" (II.B) in Figure 2.

The "control" category in Figure 2 addresses the question of who finally decides on the directions and procedures; the "orientation" category concerns the dominant source of

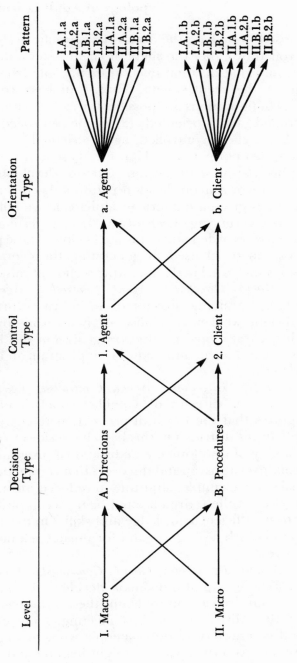

Figure 2. Patterns of Decision Control Orientation

| Level | Decision Type | Control Type | Orientation Type | Pattern |

data used in making the decision. A specific decision may be controlled by either the agent or client system; the dominant input into that decision may, in turn, come from either the agent or the client system. Thus, four basic control-orientation configurations are possible for each decision: (1) agent controlled, agent oriented; (2) agent controlled, client oriented; (3) client controlled, agent oriented; (4) client controlled, client oriented. In Figure 2, these four configurations have been applied to the four types of developmental decisions to form sixteen decision patterns. Each component of Figure 2 is given a numeric or alphabetic symbol for ease of pattern referencing. Each of the sixteen resultant decision patterns is recorded and explicated below. These patterns are the raw material used in generating the overall program typology discussed in the following section of this chapter.

Macro Directions: Agent Controlled, Agent Oriented (I.A.1.a). A training director of an industrial firm identifies insufficient worker capability as the reason for failure to reach organizational production goals. On this basis he decides to conduct an adult education program and formulates its objectives.

Macro Directions: Agent Controlled, Client Oriented (I.A.1.b). The director of a public school evening division recognizes that there is a disproportionate share of retired people in his district. On this basis he decides to explore the desirability of developing an educational program for them. He conducts a survey and discovers that certain developmental tasks (for example, adjusting to reduced income or death of spouse) of the retired are not being accomplished, due in part to insufficient knowledge and skill. On this basis he decides to launch a program and formulates relevant program objectives.

Macro Directions: Client Controlled, Agent Oriented (I.A.2.a). A group of individuals decide to form a neighborhood group to learn more about the community issues that affect their lives. At the first meeting, members consider several community resource people who, by organizational position or known capability, might help them decide on the most crucial issues to explore. An educator from a university is selected and invited to the next meeting to identify and explicate crucial community issues. On the basis of information thus received, the group selects the issues with which it intends to deal.

Macro Directions: Client Controlled, Client Oriented (I.A.2.b). An individual decides to devote one hour each day to self-improvement outside of his professional interest area. He is fascinated by the fine vegetable garden in the next block and wishes to have an equally fine garden, but he is aware that he lacks the capability to plant and care for such a garden. He finally decides to spend his one hour each day for two weeks acquiring that capability.

Macro Procedures: Agent Controlled, Agent Oriented (I.B.1.a). The director of a university extension division contracts with a professional association to offer an update program for its members. The director insists that the financial arrangements be cost plus 10 percent and that the program be offered on campus using a workshop format. The director's insistence is based on his division policy of financial independence and his commitment to fully utilize the university's physical and human resources.

Macro Procedures: Agent Controlled, Client Oriented (I.B.l.b). The United States Office of Education decides to conduct a program to train trainers of adult basic education counselors, supervisors, and teachers. Recognizing the geographic dispersion of clients and their limited financial commitment to the task, the USOE decides to conduct several regional and state institutes and pay for all institute costs and client expenses.

Macro Procedures: Client Controlled, Agent Oriented (I.B.2.a). The person referred to above who decided to learn how to plant and care for a vegetable garden further decides to enroll in a class on gardening offered by the local community college, in spite of the fact that the class is scheduled at an inconvenient time and location.

Macro Procedures: Client Controlled, Client Oriented (I.B.2.b). Altering the previous example, imagine the individual deliberately considering his time and space constraints and exploring different learning resource options open to him. Further imagine him finally going to the library and checking out a number of books on gardening or simply consulting a neighbor.

Micro Directions: Agent Controlled, Agent Oriented (II.A.1.a). An adult basic education teacher specifies learning objectives on the basis of grade performance standards adopted by his school system. For another example, a training director defines learning objectives on the basis of job performance standards set by his company.

Micro Directions: Agent Controlled, Client Oriented (II.A.1.b). The educational program committee of the local chamber of commerce, after conducting a survey of member interests, conducts a lecture series to help all members learn precisely how they can conserve energy through proper use of home appliances.

Micro Directions: Client Controlled, Agent Oriented (II.A.2.a). A teacher of a metal-working class for adults presents several learning task options that fall within the boundaries of his own capability and the resources of his organization. His adult students then decide which tasks they wish to pursue.

Micro Directions: Client Controlled, Client Oriented (II.A.2.b). A council made up of directors of adult education from a variety of community agencies conducts several self-assessment exercises. The directors finally decide that their common and most crucial learning need is the knowledge and skills necessary to conduct a comprehensive community need assessment. More specifically, they decide to learn more about sources of community data and strategies for retrieving it.

Micro Procedures: Agent Controlled, Agent Oriented (II.B.1.a). A teacher in a high school completion class limits himself to techniques that involve only one-way communications. His decision is based primarily on his long-time commitment to this style and is made in spite of the fact that his students tend to be active in style and capable of sharing valuable experience.

Micro Procedures: Agent Controlled, Client Oriented (II.B.1.b). A professor conducts a workshop for professional staff of a community college. He decides to use an array of techniques and devices that would actively involve his learners. He makes this decision based on what he knows about the attention span of adult learners and the propensity of professional groups to share their experiences.

Micro Procedures: Client Controlled, Agent Oriented (II.B.2.a). Faculty of an academic department of a university decide to improve their ability to formulate goals. They decide to do this by individual study and discussion rather than by lecture from an outside authority. They base their decision primarily on the university's budget constraints.

Micro Procedures: Client Controlled, Client Oriented (II.B.2.b). A community development council conducts a survey to determine citizen preferences with respect to means of information dissemination. The results showed an overwhelming preference for panel presentations over educational television. The council, as representative of the larger community client system, decides to use a television panel to deliver facts on community crime and its control.

Program Types

Adult education programs result from various combinations of the sixteen control-orientation decision patterns just explicated. The total number of possible combinations is quite large. The purpose of this section is to develop and apply a strategy which, through numeric means, will greatly reduce the number of program types.

Numeric Formulation

Pattern reduction is essentially a matter of assigning relative numeric value to the elements of Figure 2 and then adding the values to derive a total program score. The value assumptions with which the numeric system will be weighted are that: (1) client control and orientation is twice as valuable as agent control and orientation; (2) macro decisions are twice as valuable as micro decisions; (3) directional decisions are equal in value to procedural decisions; and (4) control as a patterning concept is equal in value to orientation as a patterning concept. It is important to recognize that the actual numeric values produced by the reduction strategy that follows will be tied to the value assumptions just made. The strategy itself is not, however. In other words, the strategy would work with other sets of value assumptions.

The process of numeric formulation is summarized in Figure 3. The figure consists of six columns. The far left column represents the four major decisions of the developmental system (macro directions, macro procedures, micro directions, micro procedures). The remaining columns deal with the process of formulating scores for each decision. Column 2 is the first element in the formula and records

Figure 3. Numeric Formulation Process

1	2	3	4	5	6	
Decisions	CS +	OS =	$NADS$ ×	LWF =	ADS	
I.A	1 or 2	1 or 2	2 – 4	2	4 – 8	
I.B	1 or 2	1 or 2	2 – 4	2	4 – 8	
II.A	1 or 2	1 or 2	2 – 4	1	2 – 4	
II.B	1 or 2	1 or 2	2 – 4	1	2 – 4	
Total Score Range	4 – 8	4 – 8	8 – 16	/////	12 – 24	= TPS

I.A, I.B, II.A, II.B = Decision Categories (see Figure 2)

CS = Control Score; client equals 2 and agent equals 1

OS = Orientation Score; client equals 2 and agent equals 1

NADS = Nonadjusted Decision Score

LWF = Level Weight Factor; macro levels (I.A and I.B) equal 2 and micro levels (II.A and II.B) equal 1

ADS = Adjusted Decision Score

TPS = Total Program Score

possible control scores (CS). Each decision may receive a score of 1 or 2 depending on whether it is agent or client dominated, respectively (see value assumption 1 listed earlier). The program orientation score (OS) is also scored 1 or 2, and the total range, like the control score range, is from four to eight. Column 4 represents possible nonadjusted decision scores (NADS)—that is, scores not adjusted for level of decision value. These scores are the sums of the orientation and control scores and may thus range from 2 to 4. The total program NADS range is from 8 to 16. Column 5 records level weighting factors (LWF) that adjust decision scores to reflect value assumption 2 above. Macro decisions (I.A) are weighted by a factor of two and micro decisions (II.A) by a factor of one. The last column represents possible adjusted decision scores (ADS), which are computed by multiplying NADS by LWF. The macro decision score may range from four to eight and the micro decision from two to four. The total ADS range is from 12 to 24 and represents the total program score (TPS).

Working through an example will facilitate understanding of how programs may be scored using the process just described. My hypothetical example is an adult basic education program. Score computations for the example are recorded in Figure 4. Macro directions are under the control of the agent system ($I.A_{cs} = 1$) and oriented to agent content commitments ($I.A_{os} = 1$). Macro procedures are agent con-

Figure 4. Numeric Formulation for Example
Adult Basic Education Program

Decisions	(C S + O S = N A D S) × L W F = A D S					
I.A	1	1	2	2	4	
I.B	2	1	3	2	6	
II.A	1	1	2	1	2	
II.B	2	1	3	1	3	
Totals	6	4	10		15	= TPS

trolled ($I.B_{cs} = 1$) but client oriented ($I.B_{os} = 2$). Micro directions are agent controlled ($II.A_{cs} = 1$) and agent oriented ($II.A_{os} = 1$). Micro procedures are agent controlled ($II.B_{cs} = 1$) and client oriented ($II.B_{os} = 2$). CO and OS scores are summed in the NADS column, weighted in the LWF column, and finally adjusted in the ADS column. As revealed in the lower-right hand cell of the table, the total score for the program is 15.

Derivation of Program Types

Reference once again to Figure 3 reveals that the total program score range is from 12 to 24, resulting in thirteen possible different program scores. This span of thirteen scores could simply be left as a continuum ranging from extremely agent centered (12) to extremely client centered (24). It could also be broken down into subranges to form types, as follows. By dividing the range of thirteen scores into approximate thirds, three subranges are formed: 12–16; 17–19; and 20–24. Thus, the midrange zone is limited to three scores, and the extreme zones include five scores each. Programs falling in the 12–16 range are called "agent centered"; those falling in the 20–24 range are called "client centered"; and finally those falling in the 17–19 range are called "eclectic." This derivation of program types completes a trilogy of systems which can now be examined in terms of their interrelationships.

Agent, Client, and Program Type Relationships

In the preceding sections, emphasis has been on defining and explicating various types of agents, clients, and programs of adult education. We turn now to a summary of the types and an exploration of relationships among them. Agent and client system relationships will be discussed first, followed by relationships between system and program types. The relational statements made should be considered propositions for research rather than principles to guide practice.

Relationships Between Agent and Client Systems

Two major categories of agent systems (leadership and operating) and two categories of client systems (membership and nonmembership) were described early in this chapter. The following propositions deal with projected relationships between the agent and client systems, beginning with general elements of the classification system and followed by those dealing with specific elements.

1. Most major agent systems are involved with ongoing in-service education of staff. In some instances these staff development or training programs are planned and conducted using internal resources; in other instances extensive use is made of external resources. In the former case, clients are classified as members of the agent system; in the latter case, clients are still members, but of a system other than the dominant agent or resource system. Thus, it can be said that major agent systems make extensive use of both internal agent and external agent membership systems in performing staff development and training functions.

2. The adult education efforts of leadership agent systems are directed primarily at members of operating agencies. Thus, the prevailing form of client system used by leadership agencies is the external agent membership system.

3. Agent systems that link themselves to client membership systems have less difficulty in securing client compliance than those which link themselves with nonmember systems.

4. In general, nonmember client systems prevail in the adult education efforts of institutional agencies and individual agents, while the member client systems prevail among voluntary associations. A few exceptions to this generalization are worth noting. Special interest agencies (a type of institutional agency) are in many instances almost exclusively concerned with membership or employee training and development. Similarly, the university (an example of a type of institutional agency) frequently links itself with members of other organizations in a nonagent membership staff development effort. Exceptions to the general rule are also found

among voluntary associations. Pressure groups and service clubs (two types of voluntary associations) in particular often link themselves educatively to nonmember systems in an effort to further their interests.

5. Among institutional agencies that use nonmember client systems, educational agencies (autonomous adult education agencies and youth education agencies) tend to use broad geographic, demographic, or interest criteria for specifying target audiences or client systems; noneducational agencies (community agencies and special interest agencies) tend to use more specific social role or need criteria. As in the case of item 4 noted earlier, there are noteworthy exceptions. For instance, museums and libraries (examples of noneducational community agencies) define their client systems using broad criteria, most often of the geographic or interest type.

6. Though various agent systems often function independently (that is, individually) in relation to particular client systems, they may also join forces to expand the scope and effectiveness of their operation. For example, councils of adult education organizations may convene to address the totality of needs and problems of a total community.

7. When voluntary associations do link themselves educationally to nonmember systems, they tend to do so out of a need to secure outside support for and acceptance of their special interest mission. Such efforts are quite common among community improvement and pressure group types of voluntary associations.

Relationships Between Agent and Client Systems and Programs

Programs were typed according to the control and orientation patterns established with respect to four major program decisions: (1) macro directions, (2) macro procedures, (3) micro directions, and (4) micro procedures. Three program types were finally stipulated: (1) agent centered, (2) client centered, and (3) eclectic. The propositions that follow explore potential relationships between those program types and agent-client systems.

1. Program decisions that are affected freely by agent and client systems require more time and energy to make but engender greater commitment to action and result in more effective programs than do those that do not allow for free input from both systems.

2. The more precise a system's effect on program decisions, the greater the likelihood that the focal point of control and orientation will rest with that system. Conversely, the more general a system's effect on program decisions, the greater the likelihood that the focal point of control and orientation will move away from that system.

3. Agent or client systems that have long-standing traditions with respect to directions or procedures tend to resist input that calls for change in those traditions.

4. Operating agencies that depend on client systems for financial support are more client oriented in their decisions than will those that are not dependent. Similarly, leadership agencies that depend on operating agencies for financial support are more operating-agency oriented in their decisions than those that are not dependent.

5. Client systems that are dependent on an agent system for symbolic or monetary reward are more agent oriented in their decisions than those that are not so dependent.

6. Where input from agent and client systems do not match, power tends to be exercised by one of the component systems to secure compliance from the other.

7. Operating agencies whose direction has been affected by legal or social mandate from leadership agencies tend to be less receptive to client input than those who operate without such mandates.

8. Programs of voluntary associations and individual agents tend to be more client oriented than programs of institutional agencies.

9. Among voluntary associations, professional associations and pressure groups tend to be more agent centered in their programs than community improvement associations and social clubs.

10. Among leadership agencies, private foundations

tend to be more agent oriented in their programs than governmental offiices.

11. Programs of individual volunteer agents tend to be more agent oriented than those of entrepreneurial agents.

12. Among institutional agencies, programs of special interest agencies tend to be more agent oriented than those of educational agencies or community service agencies.

13. Membership client systems tend to be more agent oriented in their decisions than nonmember client systems.

14. Decision control and orientation patterns tend toward uniformity. For example, if macro decisions are controlled by and oriented toward the agent system, there would be a tendency toward micro decisions to likewise be controlled by and oriented toward the agent system.

Summary

This chapter has established a typology of important components of the field of adult education. Toward this end, adult education has been viewed as a developmental process used to link various agent and adult client systems for the purpose of establishing directions and procedures for programs of adult learning. Figure 5 will assist in recalling the processes. First, leadership and operating agent systems were typed, followed by the typing of membership and nonmembership client systems. Then a developmental system was generated, in which four major program decisions received potential influence from various classes of input variables from agent and client systems. Input, in turn, was viewed as being mediated by established patterns of control and orientation. Four basic patterns were stipulated and applied to the four major decisions of the system, forming a total of sixteen control-orientation patterns. By assigning relative numeric value to elements of the system, decision pattern combinations or program types were reduced to three: agent controlled, client controlled, and eclectic. Finally, agent, client, and program type relationships were explored in terms of propositions for use in further research.

Figure 5. Global Typological System

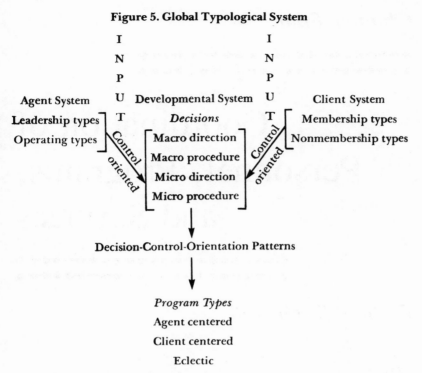

Decision-Control-Orientation Patterns

Program Types
Agent centered
Client centered
Eclectic

To perceive order in the field of adult education is indeed no simple task. To most observers, finding the patterns is as difficult as interpreting abstract modern art. Yet, by focusing on the underlying dynamics, a reflective analyst can perceive an organizational logic, a process that may not appeal to those who are content to admire the rich profusion of institutional forms in the field. I trust that the pattern that has resulted has not destroyed the field's beauty. Further, I hope the resulting pattern will raise questions which, when pursued, will increase understanding of the field. My recommendation to those concerned with adult education as a body of knowledge is that they first develop valid and reliable instruments to measure the variables implicit in the categories and types of adult education discussed in this chapter and then test the propositions that result.

◆◆◆◆◆◆◆◆◆◆◆◆◆◆◆◆◆◆◆◆◆◆◆◆◆
◆◆◆◆◆◆◆◆◆◆◆◆◆◆◆◆◆◆◆◆◆◆◆

Coordination of Personnel, Programs, and Services

◆◆◆◆◆◆◆◆◆◆◆◆◆◆◆◆◆◆◆◆◆◆◆◆◆
◆◆◆◆◆◆◆◆◆◆◆◆◆◆◆◆◆◆◆◆◆◆◆

William S. Griffith

As Malcolm Knowles noted in Chapter Two, adult education institutions seem to arise spontaneously, without regard to a grand plan and often without much consideration of existing institutional forms. He also noted that the flexibility provided by this proliferation of new forms to serve newly perceived needs constitutes a remarkably effective natural system. Even without a grand plan, institutions arise and work out accommodations with those already in existence. This natural accommodation might be considered a key idea in systems theory which, as Peters pointed out in Chapter One, may offer a useful conceptual device for finding order in the evolving structure of adult education. Peters' examples, however, focus on individual associations rather than attempting the formidable task of handling the entire field. Yet, if adult education is to become more than the sum of its individual institutions, organizations, and agencies, then adult educators will have to address the question of the coordination of the field.

This chapter will consider the current state of coordination in the field of adult education. Illustrations drawn from several countries and international bodies reveal the pervasiveness of concern for coordination. These efforts to achieve coordination at the international, regional, national, state, and local levels provide evidence of the importance of the problem and indicate that the search for viable mechanisms to accomplish coordination is still at an early stage.

Defining a Coordinated Field

Adult educators have a propensity for establishing new organizations and setting up special interest subunits of existing organizations to deal with emerging concerns. These new organizations may be of two types: those composed of individual members who represent only themselves and those composed of individuals who are representing institutions. At a higher level there are associations of representatives of both types of organizations. These higher-level associations are often founded in an attempt to overcome the natural divisiveness resulting from the formation of the narrowly focused special interest groups.

This continuous generation of new organizations produces a rich diversity of forms but simultaneously complicates the task of achieving any planned coordination among them. Of course, it might be argued that there is no need to substitute a consciously designed system of coordination for the natural coordination that already exists—that the independent efforts of the separate organizations constitute an adaptive natural system that exhibits the characteristics of spontaneity, creativity, and freedom from the repressive aspects of tradition that inhibit the adaptation of established institutions to environmental changes. New organizations arise spontaneously, it might be said, as an intuitive response to changing perceptions of needs. This uncontrolled and un-coordinated development of different aspects of the field may facilitate the expression of maximum responsiveness and exhibit a sensitivity to emerging conditions that is atypi-cal of established institutions.

Yet to the perceptive observer, the existing system is not entirely a natural one, free of controlling influences at international, regional, national, state, and local levels. If there is a choice to be made, it is not between a completely free system and one that is entirely controlled. Rather, the choice is either to accept the present part-governmental, part-private arrangements—allow them to continue to grow somewhat opportunistically—or attempt to modify the exist-ing arrangements to make them more readily accessible to adult learners and more rational, effective, and efficient in pursuing selected goals. This chapter will examine the arguments for and functions of coordinating bodies, review selected experiences with different levels of and approaches to coordination in the United States and elsewhere, and con-clude with generalizations that may be inferred from the data.

The extent to which adult education is perceived as coordinated is partly a function of the breadth of the defini-tion of the field of adult education itself. Knowles (1977) feels that the lack of agreement on a comprehensive map or defi-nition of the field has been one of the most formidable ob-stacles to coordination. Where adult education is regarded as synonymous with adult basic education, the task of coordinat-ing resources is much smaller and appreciably less involved than where the field is broadly defined. Some people may regard the task of defining adult education as nothing more than an academic exercise. In fact, however, no other step is more basic, because such definition not only indicates the scope of concerns but also establishes the range of institu-tions, agencies, organizations, and associations that must be included in a coordinated system. In this chapter the focus is on adult education, defined broadly as Knowles and Schroeder have defined it in Chapters Two and Three.

Proliferation of Adult Education Organizations

Adult educators in general—and adult educators in the United States in particular—have a peculiar predilection for establishing organizations on the basis of some narrowly defined common interest and then, driven by an apparent desire to increase the size and influence of the new group, to broaden the basis of membership even at the cost of deemphasizing the original objectives of the organization. Over the past quarter century, American adult educators have founded a number of special interest organizations that subsequently have lost their distinctive character in a quest for increased visibility and power. For example, the National Association for Public School Adult Education (NAPSAE) emerged in 1952 as a special interest group within the Adult Education Association of the United States of America (AEA) with a narrow concern for the practical operation of adult education within the public schools. Because of its primary concern with a single institutional form—the public school—NAPSAE became an affiliate of the National Education Association (NEA) in 1956. NAPSAE's affiliate status with AEA was terminated in 1963, realigning public school adult educators with elementary and secondary educators in the NEA.

The leaders of NAPSAE observed that as the community colleges proliferated, they were employing more and more adult educators, some of whom had been in public school adult education and who were continuing to look to NAPSAE as their professional organization. Throughout the 1960s, adult education in the community colleges was increasing more rapidly than it was in the public schools. Individuals who had been working in adult education in the school districts were attracted to the working conditions, salaries, and status associated with college employment; some of those who transferred to junior college teaching were not interested in continuing their identification with the public schools. The NAPSAE, in order to increase its attractiveness to community college adult educators, changed its name to the National Association for Public Continuing and Adult Education (NAPCAE), thereby blurring its previous focus on the public schools.

A similar name change occurred when the National Community School Education Association dropped the word *school* from its name, not only reflecting an evolution in the concept and definition of community education but also displaying an awareness of the growing importance of potential members who were employed by community colleges to work in community education.

Within the American Association of Community and Junior Colleges (AACJC), adult education interests have also been dynamic, if not always coordinated. With the support of a grant from the W. K. Kellogg Foundation, the AACJC established a National Council on Community Services (NCCS), which drew its membership from the flexibly defined field of community services. Following the expiration of the grant, the council exhibited the expansionistic tendency observed in other adult education organizations and changed its name to the National Council on Community Services and Continuing Education (NCCSCE). At the same time, the AACJC, fully cognizant of the federal legislative developments in community education, secured a grant from the Mott Foundation to establish a community education project, which was not integrated with the NCCSCE. This is an instance of the tendency of adult educators and adult education activities to be fractionized even within a single national organization composed entirely of individuals employed in a single type of institution.

Because of this tendency of adult educators to establish new associations and organizations, the task of developing effective coordinating bodies is especially perplexing. Existing organizations spawn independent subgroups that pursue an independent existence, and new organizations spring up like mushrooms. In an attempt to counter these separatist tendencies and to embrace the diversity of interests in the field, the NAPCAE is fostering the establishment of affiliate subdivisions. Two potentially independent and presently influential affiliated organizations are the National Council of State Directors of Adult Education (NCSDAE) and the National Council of Urban Administrators of Adult Education (NCUAAE). The NCUAAE was formed in Detroit at a meeting of approximately sixty administrators of urban adult education who felt the need for an organization that would address itself exclusively to their needs. In its constitution and by-laws, adopted May 11, 1972, the NCUAAE identified its goals and committed itself to affiliate status within NAPCAE. Perhaps the NCSDAE and the NCUAAE will remain satisfied with the scope of their membership and their affiliate status within NAPCAE. If they do, it may be useful to examine the situation for its possible utility as a model for organizing diverse special interest groups of adult educators within a single multipurpose association.

Eighteen years ago, Knowles (1977) noted that the marginal status of adult educators within the institutions that employ them induces adult educators to seek mutual support, status, and problem-solving help across institutional lines. This search for like-minded individuals to support newly defined positions in some narrow sector of the adult education field partially explains the tendency to establish associations. The inability to act as authorized representatives of their employing institutions limits the discussions and decisions of members of adult education organizations to commitments they can make as individuals. Lacking the authority to commit their institutions to any plan of action, adult educators can only discuss the need for or advantages of coordinated approaches; they cannot pledge their institution's resources to any joint agreements. If binding agreements are to be made among institutions regarding the use of their resources, such agreements can only be executed by individuals with the authority to engage in contracts on behalf of their institutions. Coordination among institutions can only be brought about by including top administrators or their official representatives in the process. Because adult education programs are only a small part of most parent institutions, the chief administrators of the institutions do not typically belong to adult education organizations, which tend, in turn, to emerge and grow in response to the perceived lack of power of the member adult educators.

National Adult Education Coordinating Bodies

In 1974, UNESCO conducted an international survey of national coordinating bodies in adult education (UNESCO, 1974). Questionnaires were sent to all member countries, and official replies were received from fifty-one government and five nongovernment respondents. Forty-one of the responding members reported that they had coordinating bodies; seven said that they were either organizing such bodies or giving serious thought to the advisability of doing so; and the following eight countries stated that they had no need for such a national coordinating organ: Belorussia, Bulgaria, Finland, Guatemala, Niger, Norway, Switzerland, and the USSR. The coordinating bodies vary widely in their purposes and responsibilities at the national level. UNESCO's interim report noted that in some instances the coordinating bodies are mostly, if not exclusively, engaged in adult literacy efforts. Nearly two thirds of the questionnaires sent by UNESCO to the national commissions were not returned, indicating a lack of systematic communications between these commissions and adult education circles in their countries. It may also reflect the low level of awareness of the importance of this aspect of adult education.

If cooperation and coordination are to be pursued as desirable means, they must be justified by the results they are expected to achieve. Under the sponsorship of the International Council for Adult Education (a voluntary international association of individual adult educators), a conference was held in England in September 1974 to examine the need for and current status of national organizations for cooperation in adult education. The conferees agreed that some national mechanism or some combination of means is required in every country and region to serve the following purposes:

1. Foster recognition and attention for the special needs and services of adult education;
2. Help link adult education to the entire educational system and learning community—adult education seen within the perspective of lifelong learning;
3. Persuade governments, intergovernmental agencies, and nongovernment organizations (NGOs) to provide more adequate resources;
4. Help establish and maintain high standards of performance;
5. Develop improved means of communication and encourage training and research; and
6. Found adult education as a response to the nation and the human family.

As the conference progressed, thirteen functions of national adult education agencies were formulated:

1. Establishing and maintaining two-way communication with the organizations and institutions inside the country that offer various forms of adult education;
2. Fostering coordination of the efforts of adult education agencies of government, nongovernment, university, and other organizations inside the country;
3. Fostering cooperation and integration of all forms of education for all ages;
4. Establishing and maintaining two-way communication with adult education interests exterior to the country, including U.N. agencies such as UNESCO, international NGOs such as the International Congress of University Adult Education, and adult education organizations in other countries;
5. Acting as an advocate on behalf of the needs and values of adult education, developing a favorable climate for adult education, and extending it to those yet unserved;

6. Examining and appraising laws, institutions, and practices in the country from the perspective of their contribution to adult education;
7. Encouraging and fostering training in adult education and the preparation and continuing education of practitioners of every kind;
8. Encouraging the development of research in adult education;
9. Encouraging the experimentation, demonstration, and refinement of methods and organization in adult education;
10. Encouraging the development of professional standards and ethical practices in adult education;
11. Identifying national social goals and their implications for adult education and fostering cooperation to achieve these goals;
12. Offering consultation and technical advice about adult education;
13. Increasing the amount and the sharing of the resources for adult education.

The conferees further described six existing types of national adult education organizations:

1. Adult education organized and administered as an integral part of the educational system, usually within a ministry of education;
2. National boards for adult education administered by the national government, such as those in Kenya, Israel, and India;
3. Major adult education agencies in the country capable of performing many national functions;
4. National nongovernmental associations, such as those in England and Canada;
5. National organizations concerned exclusively with work for adult literacy. (The Arab states, in particular, because of their desire to reduce their high illiteracy rates, have focused their efforts in this direction to the extent that

literacy work is commonly thought to be synonymous with adult education.)
6. Associations of professional or full-time practitioners, which provide many of the services of a national organization. Examples can be found in Eastern Europe and Venezuela.

The conferees clearly had in mind an ideal rather than an existing form of organization, for at present one cannot find any one of the six forms of organization carrying out all of the thirteen functions. Nevertheless the concern for improving the coordination of adult education continues to be of interest to both national and international bodies.

Various Perspectives on Coordination

UNESCO, the Organization for Economic Cooperation and Development (OECD), and a number of national and regional bodies have issued statements that reveal different perspectives on coordination and the relationship of a coordinated adult education program to a plan for national development. In order to appreciate these different perspectives, we will examine the UNESCO and OECD statements and the positions of England and Wales, Scotland, and Denmark, and then turn to examples of positions taken by groups of adult educators from countries in the Third World.

The UNESCO Perspective

The draft recommendation on the development of adult education prepared by UNESCO in August 1976, in preparation for the Nairobi General Conference Session held in October–November 1976, placed strong emphasis on coordination within the adult education field and between adult education and all other aspects of the educational system involved in life-long education and learning. The recommendations encourage member countries to endeavor to ensure the establishment, maintenance, and continuing development of a network of bodies which seek to meet the needs for adult education.

Five objectives were identified as essential elements in the development of a network:

> (1) identify and anticipate educational needs capable of being satisfied through adult education programmes;
> (2) make full use of existing educational facilities and create such facilities as may be lacking to meet all defined objectives:
> (3) make the necessary long-term investments for the development of adult education: in particular for the professional education of planners, administrators, those who train educators, organizational and training personnel, the preparation of educational strategies and methods suitable for adults, the provision of capital facilities, the production and provision of the necessary basic equipment such as visual aids, apparatus, and technical media;
> (4) encourage exchanges of experience and compile and disseminate statistical and other information on the strategies, structures, content, methods, and results, both quantitative and qualitative, of adult education;
> (5) abolish economic and social obstacles to participation in adult education, and to systematically bring the nature and form of adult education programmes to the attention of all potential beneficiaries, but especially to the most disadvantaged, by using such means as active canvassing by adult education institutions and voluntary organizations, to inform, counsel, and encourage possible and often hesitant participants in adult education [UNESCO, 1976, p. 8].

The Draft Recommendation further urged that "there should be set up, at all levels, international, regional, national and local, (1) structures or procedures for consultation and coordination between public authorities which are competent in the field of adult education; and (2) structures or procedures for consultation, coordination, and harmonization between the said public authorities, the representatives of adult learners, and the entire range of bodies carrying out adult education programmes or activities designed to promote the development of such programmes."

Even though the field of adult education, broadly defined, is itself only minimally coordinated, UNESCO seeks to encourage the coordination of adult education within a broader framework of lifelong learning rather than concentrating on tidying up the adult education field prior to seeking coordination on a grander scale. The Draft Recommendation stated as a guideline that "adult education and other forms of education, particularly school and higher education and vocational training, should be conceived and organized as equally essential components in a coordinated but differentiated education system according to the tenets of lifelong education and learning" (UNESCO, 1976, p. 4).

The UNESCO perspective is heavily influenced by the interests of the developing nations. In contrast, the Organization for Economic Cooperation and Development is primarily concerned with the industrialized nations.

The OECD Perspective

In May 1976, the OECD published a report on comprehensive policies for adult education in which it concluded that, in countries where the central educational administration is not charged with the full responsibility for adult education, the only way to ensure that a broad spectrum of learning needs will be met and that unnecessary duplication will be avoided is to establish a statutory board or council. The membership of such a council, OECD suggests, should include representatives of government departments, major adult education agencies, employers, trade unions, and public services such as broadcasting and libraries. If the system is to work effectively at all levels, similar councils would also be required to facilitate coordination at regional and local levels.

After outlining the prerequisites for a fully developed adult education system, the OECD identified four potential paths of development of adult education in OECD countries:

> (1) to let it evolve, as in the past, in a spontaneous and sporadic fashion without reference to any explicit public intervention;
> (2) to strengthen and coordinate the existing range of activities but not to perceive it as an active instrument of public policy in the social and economic arenas;
> (3) to strengthen and coordinate the existing range of activities while simultaneously pursuing a positive policy of support for specific activities judged to be national priorities, for example, secondary education equivalency programmes designed to promote equality; and
> (4) to create a comprehensive service of adult education as an integral element of broadly conceived educational systems and to relate its functions to the social, economic, and cultural objectives of the nation [OECD, 1976, p. 34].

The OECD report on comprehensive policies asserts that in the absence of government intervention there is no reason to expect adult education to respond effectively to collective local and national needs or to appeal to all sectors of society. In fact, four specific conditions are essential for the development of adult education as an instrument of public policy:

> (1) establish a comprehensive and coordinated pluralistic service commanding ample public resources;
> (2) relate its functions to such national social concerns as an active manpower policy and the quality of life;
> (3) integrate the formal (academic) and occupational training sector with regular education as part and parcel of a recurrent education system; and
> (4) initiate extraordinary measures to identify and satisfy unmet educational needs, not least those of persons adjudged to be disadvantaged [OECD, 1976, pp. 34–35].

The reason these statements on coordination and national policies are so general may be that they constitute policy recommendations rather than practical steps in an implementation process. Without effective national experiences to serve as models, the process of constructing or devising such a model is most likely to be conceptualized and described at an abstract level.

In November 1975, the Education Committee of OECD saw adult education as an indispensable part of a contemporary culture. The committee stated that "the provision of a well-endowed nationwide adult education service has become an essential policy requirement in all modern societies for both social and economic as well as cultural reasons. A dynamic adult education service is essential in enabling societies as well as individuals to adapt to the effects of rapid change, for in order that change may occur without disruptive conflicts and at a reasonable tempo, it is necessary for adults not merely to react to policies planned from above but to become, on their own initiative, participants in the evolutionary process" (OECD, 1975, p. 1).

Perspectives in Scotland and in England and Wales

Within the last decade, committees of inquiry have examined the provisions for adult education in Scotland and in England and Wales. In Scotland, the committee popularly known as the Alexander Committee was appointed "to consider the aims appropriate to voluntary leisure time courses for adults which are educational, but not specifically vocational; to examine the extent to which these are being achieved at present; and, with due regard to the need to use available resources most effectively, to make recommendations" (Scottish Institute of Adult Education, 1975, p. 6). In England and Wales, the committee popularly known as the Russell Committee was appointed "to assess the need for and to review the provision of nonvocational adult education in England and Wales; to consider the appropriateness of existing educational, administrative, and financial policies; and to make recommendations with a view to obtaining the most effective and economical deployment of available resources to enable adult education to make its proper contribution to the national system of education conceived of as a process continuing through life" (Committee of Inquiry Appointed by the Secretary of State for Education and Science, 1972, p. v.).

The Alexander Committee in Scotland endorsed the policy of continuing to vest statutory responsibility for adult education solely with the education authorities because they have been the main providers of education, they alone of the agencies involved deploy the wealth and variety of resources required for large-scale development, and they are uniquely situated to ensure the continuity of educational opportunity which the future demands. Although the local education authorities were expected to retain the preeminent role in the provision of expanding opportunities for adult education, they were advised to increase their cooperation in order to make more effective use of the resources and expertise of the nongovernment organizations.

The Russell Committee rejected the notion that local education authorities (LEAs) should be the sole providers of government subsidized adult education in England and Wales. The committee felt that it was important to take advantage of the "enterprise and accumulated experience" of the voluntary bodies. They also believed that local units of national voluntary bodies were able to bring a wide vision and impart a freshness and flexibility that might be lacking in programming efforts of a purely local nature. Also, it was recognized that voluntary agencies contribute resources far in excess of the share paid by limited public grants. Finally the committee observed that voluntary organizations can conduct educational work in controversial fields more readily than statutory bodies. The committee asserted "adult education is emasculated if it cannot venture into areas of social, political, industrial, religious, or moral controversy: the right to do so is implicit in the word 'adult.' Boldness in these matters is often easier for voluntary organizations" (Committee of Inquiry Appointed by the Secretary of State for Education and Science, 1972, pp. 50–51).

The Russell Report also called for the establishment of a Development Council for England and Wales and a Local Development Council in every local education area. The Development Council for England and Wales is to consist of elected officials and professional adult educators appointed by the Secretary of State for Education and Science. This council is to be responsible for monitoring the development and functioning of adult education and to recommend national policies to the secretary regarding identification of needs, changes of priority, and encouragement of new developments, including curriculum development, expansion of existing facilities, supply and training of staff, improvement of accommodation and equipment, joint use of educational plant, and appropriate research.

The Local Development Councils for adult education are to be representative of parties with an interest in adult education as providers or users and are to be drawn from the major providing bodies; the educational and quasi-educational institutions; associations of tutors and teachers, industry, voluntary, social, and community organizations; associations for the disadvantaged; local radio; local societies; students' councils of adult education institutions; and similar bodies. The Local Development Councils for Adult Education are to be fairly large bodies in order to involve the wide range of contributory interests in the planning and to provide evidence to all concerned that adult education truly permeates the entire life of the community (Committee of Inquiry Appointed by the Secretary of State for Education and Science, 1972). No financial powers are to be delegated to the local councils. Instead their three major functions are to be: (1) to facilitate discussion and consultation among all those interested in adult education so as to review and influence the planning of adult education in the area; (2) to ensure that needs are met and that full advantage is taken of the cultural and educational resources of the area; and (3) to indicate areas in which program is inadequate and to sponsor or suggest experiments.

In providing for adequate adult education locally, the Russell Committee strongly endorsed direct grants from the central government because they are only a contribution toward a larger total expenditure; they remove some of the program operators' financial anxiety, leaving them somewhat freer to concentrate on improving the effectiveness of their programs; and finally, without such subvention some providing bodies would withdraw from the field because their income from all other sources would fall short of covering their expenses. In short, the Russell Committee endorsed the principle of multiple providing bodies in adult education, not only because multiple providing bodies are conducive to the operation of adult education programs dealing with the full range of human concerns but also because fewer public funds are required to support such programs than would be the case if all programming were to be conducted by government bodies.

The Perspective in Denmark

In Denmark, Himmelstrup (1976) observed that the lack of a coordinated adult education system confuses prospective learners, who form their impressions of learning opportunities from the advertisements they see and the mailed circulars they receive. Because the consumers of adult education have imperfect knowledge of learning opportunities and supportive services, they are unable to make the most efficient use of the existing system. Himmelstrup believes that an improved public information system for adult education would increase its efficiency and would indirectly improve coordination among the providing bodies.

The Perspective of Third World Countries

The task of improving coordination among the providing bodies is, in one sense, the same task in all countries. If the situation is examined somewhat more closely, however, it is apparent that the industrialized nations, because of their greater total and per capita wealth, are better able to afford duplication and the uncoordinated use of resources than are the developing nations. In a country where there is a low literacy rate, low per capita income, few voluntary agencies of adult education, a public school system that reaches only a minority of children and youth, and a government that is greatly concerned with stimulating and assisting development, there is an understandable desire to avoid wasting any scarce resources in maintaining an uncoordinated system for providing educational opportunities for adults.

A seminar to examine the organization of adult education in developing countries was held in 1975 by the African Adult Education Association, the International Congress on University Adult Education, the International Council for Adult Education, and UNESCO. The conferees' concern for coordination is reflected in their recommendations: "a close working relationship should be established between the statutory and nonstatutory agencies so that all the resources available can be used in a coordinated and cooperative manner to the greatest benefit of the community as a whole; . . . a relationship of mutual assistance should be fostered between the formal system of education and adult education; . . . effective administrative structures should be established for adult education extending from the national to local levels" (African Adult Education Association, 1975, pp. 11, 12, 16).

Not all of the participants in the seminar believed that coordinating bodies should have the power to dictate to the providing bodies. Some believed that the coordination should be separated from control and should allow considerable freedom for individual institutions to develop whatever programs they chose. Many feared that a controlling body would discourage new groups from attempting to enter the field. Although the coordinating body might play a major role in determining how government grants would be allocated, the participants believed that the power of such a body should not extend to the specification of areas of activity that were not dependent upon governmental subsidization.

Experience with ministries of education that control adult education led to several observations. First, when overall responsibility for the provision of adult education rests with a ministry of education, it is the rule rather than the exception for expenditures on adult education to be regarded as marginal to the prior claims of the formal system. To guard against the diversion of funds intended for adult education to the support of the formal system, it has been found advisable to earmark the appropriation to the education ministry so that adult education is assured of receiving support within a stipulated percentage range of the education budget.

It appears axiomatic that a ministry of education must carry a major share of the responsibility for providing adult education. The problem, then, is how the government can encourage coordinated adult education provision by other government ministries and by nongovernment organizations as well. Experience in Africa leads to the conclusion that coordination is best achieved by the establishment of a statutory board that represents a variety of minstries and other organizations but does not have fiscal control.

Participants in the seminar felt that many well-intentioned attempts to strengthen adult education have been unsuccessful because they have been limited to a few component areas of adult education and because the need to ensure corresponding development of the other components has been overlooked. The seminar concluded that only by taking a comprehensive view of the field of adult education—that is, by regarding it as a system of apparently independent but in fact interacting components, each either supporting or weakening the others—will it be possible to achieve a harmonious development of the whole and produce a significant and lasting development of adult education (African Adult Education Association, 1975, p. 16).

Having examined the opinions on coordination of adult education in European and third-world countries, we now shift our focus back to the United States.

Adult Education in the U.S.

James R. Dorland, Executive Director of the National Association for Public Continuing and Adult Education and past chairman of the Coalition of Adult Education Organizations (CAEO), has concluded that the existence of so many associations that do not work together effectively partially explains the lack of influence of adult educators:

> Adult education as a movement and as a profession has been organized and governed in such an uncoordinated fashion and with such a lack of visible unity that its impact on the public school system or upon any other major institution has been and continues to be greatly diffused. On behalf of K-12 education, primarily, the National Education Association speaks with a loud, clear voice. The American Council on Education convincingly articulates the cause for higher education. The American Vocational Association strongly represents the field of vocational education. However, the various groups who are committed to the cause of lifelong learning exist almost independently of each other and in far too many instances do not coordinate their activities or work out methods by which together they could more effectively represent continuing education [Dorland, 1976, p. 391].

This observation is particularly significant in light of the fact that the CAEO was established by national associations of adult educators specifically to facilitate cooperation and coordination.

The CAEO

The Coalition of Adult Education Organizations (CAEO) was founded in 1969 and functioned as an ad hoc group until 1973, when it became incorporated to serve the following purposes:

1. To identify and focus on major issues in adult and continuing education;
2. To facilitate the exchange of information about resources, actions, and plans of its member organizations;

3. To facilitate the exchange of information about various aspects of adult and continuing education, including programs, financial support, legislation, administration, professional development, publications, research, and selection of faculty and staff;
4. To facilitate joint planning of projects to serve the field of adult and continuing education;
5. To be a resource for information and consultative services concerning adult and continuing education;
6. To promote the support of governments, foundations, and agencies to achieve equal educational opportunity for all persons; and
7. To cooperate with other groups, agencies, and organizations in the achievement of these goals.

The majority of adult educators have never even heard of the eleven-year-old CAEO. Its accomplishments have not been publicized even to members of the organizations that compose it, and its influence is slight. The number of member organizations is increasing gradually, so the coalition may yet develop into a significant center of influence in adult education. There seems to be little reason to predict that its development and role in the future will be very different from its rather inauspicious past. Inadequate though it may be for the challenges of the last quarter of the twentieth century, the CAEO is presently the only national instrument in the field of adult education, and it is on this foundation that leaders of the adult education profession must design their structure for coordinated action in the future.

One of the ways in which the CAEO has attempted to improve the coordination of adult education in the United States has been to convene invitational seminars to produce a common definition of problems and to attempt to encourage a commitment to a common set of operating principles or goals. One such conference held in 1976 produced, among other outcomes, a set of new imperatives, some of which deal with coordination: "(6) to expand services for information referral and counseling for adult learners. . . . (11) To

bring about better utilization and coordination of resources
—human, fiscal, programmatic—in the field of adult education. (12) To develop appropriate perspectives and relationships between government agencies—federal, state, local—
and the various elements of the adult education community.
(13) To encourage continuing interaction among and cooperation of, national organizations concerned with learning
for adults" ("New Imperatives Drafted at Wingspread,"
1976, pp. 1–2).

What remains unclear is the assumed mechanism for
accomplishing these imperatives. Although a great many
organizations profess a concern for improving coordination
and cooperation, it is quite another matter to expand institutional resources to develop and operate coordinative mechanisms. While there is no organized opposition to the idea
of improving coordination, neither is there a willingness to
devote institutional resources to this purpose.

Initiatives have been and continue to be taken by
national organizations (singly and collectively), by federal
government bodies, and by state-level government and nongovernment organizations to facilitate coordination. Only a
few of the many activities in this area can be mentioned, but
they are indicative of the concern being expressed throughout the nation.

Other Attempts to Coordinate the Field

The theme of the NAPCAE's 1975 national conference was "Striving for Synergy in Adult Education." The
term *synergy* was adopted from the field of biology, where it
is used to define the joint effect produced by two entities
functioning together, which is greater than the effects that
would be produced if each entity functioned separately. At
this conference, emphasis was placed on the identification
and analysis of the advantages and disadvantages of increasing collaborative efforts. The presidents or presidents-elect
of six major national associations of adult educators participated in a panel discussion of the theme at one general

session. The chief staff members of four federal advisory councils dealing with adult education also spoke to the conference theme in a general session. These advisory councils, which routinely inform, advise, and make recommendations to the executive branch of the national government, are in a strategic position to focus attention on adult education concerns and at present may have more influence on federal adult education policies than is exercised by the numerous associations working in the field. One panelist mentioned that although all four councils have offices near each other in Washington, D.C., the four staff leaders had never previously met to discuss their common concern for the role of federal policies and programs in increasing and improving adult education. These staff members acknowledged that little attention had been given by any one council to the work of the others. Further, they all agreed that consultation and collaboration among them would yield advantages to all.

When cooperation for mutual benefit is the theme of a national annual conference, the idea of cooperation gains momentary attention, and speakers can be expected to make favorable comments about it. But cooperation is a day-to-day commitment, involving routine consultation with others as individuals and associations conduct their regular business and promote their special interests. If association officers and advisory council staff members are committed to increasing their cooperative efforts, this commitment will become visible to the general membership and, of equal or greater importance, to the Department of Education and to the members of Congress.

Myriad agencies that conduct, promote, and support adult education exist within the federal government. The U.S. National Advisory Council on Extension and Continuing Education found that no effective mechanism has yet been developed through which federal agencies can coordinate and better utilize their continuing education resources (U.S. National Advisory Council on Extension and Continuing Education, 1976, p. 4). A Federal Interagency Committee on Education (FICE) has been developed, but it has yet to propose a design for the coordination of education conducted and sponsored by the national government.

The National Advisory Council on Adult Education (formerly the National Advisory Council on Adult Basic Education) has been attempting to stimulate the development of a coherent national policy for adult education. One of its ambitions is to hold a national conference to examine the problems of lifelong learning and to provide suggestions for Congress to use in formulating federal policy.

Federal Efforts. Congressional intentions regarding the coordination of adult education activities are reflected in Part B, Title I of the Education Amendments of 1976 (P.L. 94-482). Congress called for more effective use of the resources of the nation's educational institutions to assist in the solution of community problems. To achieve the goals of the act, Congress provided an impressive list of functions for the Assistant Secretary of Health, Education, and Welfare. One of these tasks is to foster improved coordination of federal support for lifelong learning programs. Another very comprehensive task is to review the lifelong learning opportunities provided through employers, unions, the media, libraries and museums, secondary schools and postsecondary educational institutions, and other public and private organizations to determine means by which their effectiveness and coordination may be enhanced and to assess, evaluate the need for, demonstrate, and develop alternative methods to improve coordination within communities among educators, employers, labor organizations, and other appropriate individuals and entities to ensure that lifelong learning opportunities are designed to meet projected career and occupational needs of the community, after considering the availability of guidance and counseling, information regarding occupational and career opportunities, and appropriate educational needs of the community.

The legislation reflects an awareness of the present lack of coordinated provisions for lifetime learning, and its passage has alerted adult education leaders to a congressional interest and to a potential source of funding for coordinated approaches to the provision of lifetime learning opportunities.

State Efforts. Adult educators in several states have developed new structures to facilitate cooperation and coordination among their associations. In Iowa and Minnesota, merger efforts have reduced the total number of associations of adult educators. In Michigan, a coalition of four adult, community, and continuing educators' associations has been formed without dissolving the component associations. This coalition makes it possible for members of each of the four specialized associations to maintain individuality, focus, and influence within the separate associations while at the time providing a consolidated platform where the many overlapping short- and long-range goals and objectives of all the organizations can be advanced in a complementary fashion (Ferrier, n.d.).

The Illinois Adult Education Association and the Public Adult and Continuing Educators' Association of Illinois, interested in increasing their political influence, established a United Coalition for Legislative Action. Because of their satisfaction with the coalition, the two associations agreed to incorporate within their membership dues an amount for the support of the coalition and to require the members of each association to become members of both by paying a standard fee to the treasurer of either organization. In 1979, the two associations adopted a common constitution to facilitate cooperation and reduce operating costs while retaining the unique features of programming that serve the special interests of the members of each group.

Not all state organizations are moving toward consolidation, however. California, which is often regarded as a bellwether for adult education, is the most conspicuous example of the opposite trend. For several years, adult educators in California public school and community college districts were members of a single statewide organization. Then, for reasons that are still debated, the common interests of the two groups in adult education became less important to them than their identification with their employing institutions.

The public school adult educators formed a special interest group within the Association of California School Administrators (ACSA), a politically alert group that tries to influence the state Department of Education and the legislature. Adult educators in the community colleges formed the California Community College Continuing Education Association, which focuses on programs of the community colleges. Apparently the forces that tend to fractionize the field of adult education continue to be almost equal in strength to those favoring coordination.

The changes in Iowa, Minnesota, Illinois, and California have been changes in the associations of adult educators. In addition to the efforts of voluntary organizations, there have been significant attempts to promote coordination through the use of state funding mechanisms. In Texas, for example, state funds are available to support adult secondary education only if the planning at the local level has been done cooperatively by all of the potential providers in the local area. In Illinois, a Task Force on Adult and Continuing Education developed a set of recommendations directed toward a coordinated approach to the provision of adult education through the secondary level (Illinois Task Force on Adult and Continuing Education, 1974). The fifteen recommendations of the task force called for a State Advisory Committee for Adult Education, broadly representative of adult education interests and accountable to a standing joint committee of the State Board of Education and the State Board of Higher Education. Local advisory councils were to be developed in each of the forty community college districts of the state to assess needs and resources, prepare a plan of operation, and submit the plan to the State Advisory Committee for review and funding. Although the recommendations have not yet been funded, the report is significant, as is the Texas plan, because it recommends the use of state funds for adult education as an incentive for institutions to coordinate their programs. No compulsion is involved—simply a mandated process of planning, which is to be followed by institutions that want to become eligible for state support.

California, which has a history of fairly liberal state support policies for adult education, has yet to find a satisfactory funding policy that will foster the development of a coordinated supply system for publicly supported adult education in the public schools and community colleges. In 1972, the California legislature enacted Senate Bill 94, mandating the establishment of area adult continuing education coordination councils. These councils, composed of representatives from community colleges and public school districts, were to meet at least quarterly to review adult education plans and offerings, to make recommendations to district boards for eliminating unnecessary duplications, to review community needs for adult and continuing education, and to recommend the appropriate level of instruction for all proposed courses. Also in 1972, the California legislature passed Senate Bills 6 and 90 as parts of a state tax reform. In an attempt to ensure the intended tax relief for property owners, the legislature moved away from the previous policy of setting limits on local property tax rates, instead placing a limit on the maximum property tax revenue that local districts could raise per unit of average daily attendance.

In May 1975, the California Department of Finance discovered that participation in adult education was growing so rapidly that the unanticipated cost to the state of average daily attendance (ADA) support to community colleges, regional occupational centers and programs, and adult education within the public schools was approaching $118 million. Because of this unexpected expense, the state would be able to increase ADA support in 1975–76 only 5 percent over the 1974–75 figure, despite projections that enrollments would increase by 9 percent (Peterson, 1975, p. 20). It was found that most of the new adult education enrollment was generating levels of state aid to local districts that exceeded the costs of conducting the programs. The new tax policy encouraged local districts to expand low-cost adult education programs as a means of increasing the total units of ADA, which, in turn, permitted the districts to increase their tax revenue. The net effect of the new tax policy turned out to be just the opposite of what the legislature had intended.

Continuing its efforts to rationalize state-supported adult education, the California legislature enacted Assembly Bill 1821, which requires each community college district to be a participant in a regional adult and vocational education council. These regional councils supplanted the adult continuing education coordination councils, but it is still too soon after their establishment to appraise their effectiveness in coordinating the provision of adult education opportunities by community college and public school districts through regional occupational centers and programs.

In California, probably to a higher degree than in any other state, competing state agencies have proliferated, with each agency hiring competent and ambitious staff members. This proliferation ensures extensive critical examinations of legislation and of the behavior of administrators in adult education. Weiner (1977) has observed that although many entities are critical of state policies and programs in adult education, there is no effective forum to discuss proposed adult education policy and to facilitate bargaining over points of disagreement. Thus, while economy-minded groups may point out the defects and apparent confusion of purposes, there has not yet been developed an effective instrument for formulating more effective legislation and regulations. Proposition 13 has further intensified the competition for funds, and the effects of the citizens' tax reform lobby in California on state and local support for adult education will be a major force in the future.

In Connecticut in 1975, a special committee examined the extent of coordination in adult education on behalf of the Commission for Higher Education. The committee called for increased consultation among institutions that provide adult education and recommended that funding sources and policy-making bodies be included in planning so that they would not inadvertently thwart coordination efforts (Resource Group on Continuing Education and Community Services, 1975).

Although commendable efforts have been made to formulate satisfactory adult education policy and to draft legislation to ensure that a coordinated rather than an entrepreneurial approach will prevail in the provision of adult education by publicly supported educational institutions, no state has been successful in developing the model legislation to accomplish this goal. Until a method is found to produce the desired coordination in the publicly supported institutions, the coordination of both public and private providers will be delayed.

Australian Experience with State-Level Coordination Boards

In Australia, various approaches have been devised to improve the coordination of adult education. Australia has four state-level adult education boards or councils to maintain and improve the provision of adult learning. In three states—Queensland, Tasmania, and Victoria—the boards are engaged in the direct provision of classes. The Queensland board has followed the policy of providing adult classes at no charge to the participants. All support for the program is provided by the state government, and the board does not (nor is it expected to) coordinate its efforts with the adult education activities of the universities, colleges, or the program conducted by the Parents' and Citizens' Committees in the local state schools. A reorganization in Queensland in 1974 placed the Adult Education Board under the control of the technical education division of the Queensland Department of Education.

In Tasmania, the board is also primarily involved in conducting programs that are planned and administered by its own staff, including staff members permanently stationed in the larger towns. Although this board cooperates with other bodies in sponsoring programs, the task of coordinating all provision for adult education in Tasmania is not regarded as an important function of the board. The Tasmanian board has also been reorganized (as of 1973), so that now it is responsible to the administrator of the Department of Education rather than directly to the Minister of Education.

The third board is known as the Council of Adult Education of Victoria, and it has a broader mandate than the Queensland and Tasmanian boards. The 1958 Education Act of the State of Victoria authorized the council to conduct programs by itself or in collaboration with any other body; to contract for concerts, recitals, exhibitions, theatrical performances, and entertainment; and to use funds under its control to support the work of local advisory councils or other bodies engaged in adult education in Victoria. As part of its effort in encouraging other providing bodies, the council produces an annual *Directory of Courses for Adults,* which lists the topic, location, entrance level, time, duration, and fee for all part-time courses for adults offered anywhere in Victoria by any agency, organization, or institution. Approximately 60 percent of the council's income is provided by the state and commonwealth governments, with the major share coming from a general state grant and only a minor portion coming from special projects supported by the Australian Commonwealth on a categorical basis.

Colin F. Cave, while serving as Director of the Victoria council, played an important leadership role in stimulating the development of adult education throughout Victoria. At his suggestion, the regional superintendent of the state education department in the Ballarat area employed a part-time assistant to facilitate the development of adult education provision by the organizations, agencies, and associations that were already involved in such work. By serving as a catalyst and by refraining from developing a competing program, the assistant was able to persuade the existing providers to participate in a combined public information program, which resulted in a three-fold increase in registrations for all of the cooperating providers. Based on their successful experience in working together, the agencies and interested members of the public established the Ballarat Regional Association for Continuing Education (BRACE), which is one of the regional councils with which the Victorian Council of Adult Education works collaboratively. The council, which provides educational and cultural opportunities where others are unable to

do so and which pursues a goal of strengthening other providing bodies by furnishing both counsel and funds, is a
noteworthy demonstration of a state-supported agency—
governed by an appointed board and responsible to the
minister for education—which steadfastly pursues the goal of
increasing and improving the provisions for adult education,
broadly defined, throughout the state.

In New South Wales, an adult education board has
seen its role as advising the state government on the dis-
tribution of its appropriations for adult education. The
board does not engage in the direct provision of services and,
except for occasional reports from its members, has not
actively pursued any activities to stimulate or to facilitate a
greater degree of cooperation and coordination among the
providing bodies than that which arises out of the initiative of
individual providers. The board was originally composed of
representatives of the organizations seeking support from
the state. In 1974 a reconstitution of this board, adding
representatives of organizations providing adult education
and of communities desiring increased service who had not
previously been represented on the board, was carried out by
the Minister of Education in an effort to increase its role in
stimulating adult education development in new organizations and in communities that previously had not been as-
sisted by the board.

The Australian experience indicates both an unusually
strong interest in adult education on the part of state
governments in four adjacent states and an acceptance of the
responsibility for attempting to provide efficient and effective
service through the appointment of a board of citizens, organizational representatives, and government officers to ensure that appropriations are spent wisely. State pride (rather
than a lack of communications among the states) has pre-
served the distinctive character of each of the four boards.

Coordination at the Community Level

Even though state governments in the United States
are able to effect coordination at the state level to some

degree, it is finally at the community level that services are provided. Effective coordination is reflected in the way that organizations relate to one another and by the manner in which the full range of adult education services is made available to the individual adult learner. Federal and state funding can be an important factor influencing the local sense of the advantages and disadvantages of working together.

Federal Funding Influence

The effects of categorical federal funding of adult basic education on the coordination of adult education at the community level was studied by Griffith and others (1974) as a part of their survey of the cost-benefit relationships in adult basic education in public schools and community colleges. These investigators observed that the guidelines for dispensing categorical funding were in effect an inducement for an entrepreneurial approach to programming. No restrictions had been placed on the way the federal funds could be distributed in local communities, and no requirements had been stipulated at the state level to ensure that those already engaged in providing adult education would be consulted on the selection of organizations that would receive the adult basic education money. Thus, the selection was made with little or no consideration of its impact on the infrastructure of adult education in local communities, and funds were assigned without systematically considering the displacement effects on the local complex of providing bodies. If appropriations are made for the Lifelong Learning Act of 1976, the guidelines for communities and organizations seeking such funds are likely to require a higher degree of community involvement in adult education decision making.

Attempts to Cope

Adult learners are the potential beneficiaries of increased cooperation and coordination in the field. Various efforts have been made at the community level by or on behalf of adult learners to assist them in coping with the uncoordinated supply of adult education.

Adult education councils have been established in several American cities over the past sixty years to help adult learners and to encourage the development of programs to satisfy unmet adult learning interests. (Knowles discussed some of these councils in Chapter Three.) These councils have had a difficult time becoming and remaining financially viable. Generally they have not enjoyed financial support from the adult education program sponsors in their communities; instead they have relied upon membership dues, contributions, and income from ancillary services such as the management of speakers' bureaus or the publication of various directories. These councils tend to exist on the borderline of insolvency, without financial support from private foundations or governments. For example, in 1975, the Adult Education Council of Greater Chicago closed down after fifty-one years of service because of mounting expenses and a declining interest in the range of services it was prepared to provide.

Verner (1962) identified three major factors influential in determining the success or failure of coordinating devices on the community level: (1) homogenity of interest, (2) clarity and acceptance of function, and (3) source of financial support. He also noted that adult education coordinating councils seem to have three chronic weaknesses: "(1) no consistent basis for adequate financial support, (2) no generally recognized identification of function, and (3) a persistent failure to achieve the sustained effective involvement and participation of local agencies concerned with educational programs for adults" (pp. 26–27). Unfortunately little progress appears to have been made since 1962.

Two new kinds of adult education facilitating organizations have been established to improve communications between those who wish to learn and those who wish to teach. One of these new organizations is called "The Learning Exchange," which describes itself as "a free and independent nonprofit community information service which links people who want to acquire knowledge and skills with those who have expertise to dispense outside the constraints of the traditional educational system" (Levy, 1975, p. 11). One of the major differences between the adult education council approach and that of the learning exchange is that the former concentrates on the traditional educational system, while the latter, based on the teaching of Ivan Illich, proudly proclaims its freedom from the established institutions and procedures.

An example of such an organization is the Evanston Learning Exchange. To join it, individuals write or telephone the exchange's office and request a registration form. They are asked to complete the form, return it, and call again a few days later to discuss their interests with a staff member. Staff members match up prospective teachers and students. The exchange gives the student the name and telephone number of a teacher, and the two of them arrange the fees, the time, and the location of the instruction. Since its establishment in 1971, the Evanston Learning Exchange has received financial support from foundations, corporations, and members' contributions. A grant from the Fund for the Improvement of Postsecondary Education supported the exchange's work in 1976–77 (Levy, 1975).

The second new kind of organization is exemplified by the National Center for Educational Brokering, situated in Syracuse, New York. The center is a nonprofit educational organization designed to promote educational brokering through technical assistance, publications, and public policy studies and recommendations. The center defines "brokering" as a service to clients through assessment, advisement, and advocacy, and by serving as an intermediary between adult learners and a variety of educational resources. Its monthly publication, the *Bulletin,* reports on the work of the center and on other organizations throughout the United States that perform similar brokering functions. Financial support for the center comes from a variety of private and public sources, including the federal Fund for the Improvement of Postsecondary Education. (This federal support is of a temporary nature, with no assurance that it will be continued.)

Whether there will be continuing federal support for

the coordination of adult education and what the level of that support will be depends largely upon the experience with two pieces of legislation. The Community Education Act calls for community-level planning, but it has not yet been funded to a degree that will affect many American communities. The Lifelong Learning Act also requires community coordination as a condition of eligibility for federal support, but its influence will not be known until Congress appropriates the funds for its implementation and communities have had some experience in following its guidelines. For both laws to be effective, it will be necessary for American communities to devise mechanisms to achieve a coordinated approach to adult education programming.

A Canadian Approach to Community-Level Coordination

The Province of Alberta is experimenting with a system of Local Further Education Councils. The seventy-five councils, which are responsible for programming in an area coterminous with local school districts, are intended to assist a community to identify local educational needs and interests and individuals who are qualified and willing to teach. Long (1976) reported that the councils are composed of representatives of such groups as the local arts council, women's institute, and churches; professionals from public agencies and institutions with responsibility for adult education; a departmental program consultant; and representatives of the local university, community college, and technical institute. With seed money provided by the provincial government, the Local Further Education Councils can provide supplemental "coordination grants" to public institutions of higher education and can also hire teachers and sponsor courses directly. The local councils were designed primarily to serve small rural communities by encouraging cooperative planning among institutions of higher education. By placing funds at the disposal of the local councils, the provincial government increases the attractiveness of rural programming to higher education institutions, which otherwise might not be inclined to serve such communities directly.

An Overview of Coordination Efforts

The need for and mechanisms of coordination for adult education have been discussed extensively by adult educators at local, state, regional, national, and international levels. Although professional adult educators may be competent to diagnose these needs and to suggest mechanisms, in most cases they are powerless to implement the recommendations they draft. It seems unlikely that adult educators who occupy subordinate positions in institutional hierarchies will be successful in persuading their superiors to enter into cooperative program agreements for the sake of some abstract notion of the common good. It is more realistic to expect that the most effective stimulus for coordination is likely to come from resource suppliers, that is local, state, and federal governments.

If a coordinated system of adult education provision is to be developed, it will most likely come about because legislators—acting on their own or in response to the compelling arguments of thoughtful and articulate adult educators—pass legislation that provides financial support to institutions that function cooperatively and denies support to those which conduct their programs in solo fashion. Inasmuch as both the federal and state governments are already deeply involved in funding a wide range of adult education programs, they are currently rewarding institutions for operating in an uncoordinated fashion. To encourage coordinated planning, programming and evaluating, it is not necessary to increase funds. Instead, changing the eligibility requirements for federal or state funding is a more economical method of stimulating an awareness of the need for a coordinated approach to the provision of adult education at the community level.

Coordination may prove to be the missing ingredient in forging an integrated and efficient system of lifelong education that will attract and serve the millions of adults who presently cannot find programs that offer a means of achieving more satisfying and rewarding lives. In the final analysis, the most important criterion for evaluating the usefulness of the coordinated provision of adult education services must be its demonstrated superiority in improving both access to and participation in the widest range of learning opportunities for the adult population.

Chapter Five

A Systems Approach
to Examining
Adult Education

John M. Peters

By now, even the casual reader will have recognized the pluralistic nature of adult education; Knowles, Schroeder, and Griffith have testified to that inescapable conclusion. However, to the serious student of adult education, this perception of an amorphous, wide-ranging array of institutions, agencies, and programs may lead to an unsettling feeling, because the field is not easily comprehensible and its processes are difficult to conceptualize.

Scholars of adult education have an additional problem. Not only must they be concerned with the plethora of organized forms of adult education, but they must also draw from a multidisciplinary knowledge base for their teaching and research activities. The behavioral sciences, the physical sciences, even the arts are tapped in the search for relevant theory, concepts, and principles. Professors and graduate students in adult education have hammered out a few propositions and assumptions about the practice of adult education to demonstrate that there is substance in the field worthy of theory-building efforts. Schroeder's concluding effort to establish a global typology in Chapter Three of this volume is a contemporary example.

Given the field's broad and varied base of practice and its multidisciplinary resource base, there remains a need for perspective or an organizing framework for further study of adult education. This chapter turns toward the potential of systems theory as one organizing framework for additional inquiry into the nature of adult education enterprises. To prepare the reader for this task, it is essential to review the process of theory building and to describe in some detail the systems approach to organizational analysis. Finally, an example of the application of systems theory to the analysis of the Adult Education Association is presented.

Theory Building

Claude Levi-Strauss, the eminent French anthropologist, retrospectively viewed his scholarly purpose as that of a theoretician, "to introduce some order into a field where knowledge was very chaotic" (*Chronicle of Higher Education,* 1978, p. 7). Anthropology, a young discipline in France when Levi-Strauss began his career, was a subfield of sociology, itself in turn a subfield of philosophy. Anthropology resembled then what adult education resembles today, except that adult education does not even enjoy the luxury of being a subset of a discipline. In fact, it may never become a discipline but may remain a field of practice within education.

Discipline or not, a recognized area of professional practice needs a knowledge base as well as guiding conceptual frameworks. Questions remain about such problematic situations as the most effective relationship between teacher and learner, the program planner and his clients, and the nature of coordinative arrangements among organizations that sponsor adult education activities. Answers to these questions must come from somewhere. Currently, the answers spring from personal and organizational experience, intuition, and the bases of knowledge found in academic disciplines and other areas of professional practice. And, although the knowledge base in adult education is certainly expanding, it is far from sufficient to deal optimally with complex problems faced by the practicing adult educator as well as the would-be scholar of adult education. The field of adult education needs further development in theory formation and development and in principles of practice. The search for ordered, systematic thinking will continue. The question is, where do we look for inspiration?

Professors of adult education and their students, most of the latter now out in "the field," are aware that studies of adult education have been and continue to be dependent on the behavioral sciences and the general area of education. These professors have surveyed the literature in these and other areas of scholastic inquiry and professional practice for resources to help us understand the enterprises of adult education and their constituencies. For example, we have tried to determine simultaneously the roles of organized forms of adult education and the nature of the adult learner for whom the organized forms were developed. The disciplines of psychology, physiology, and sociology, among others, have served us well in clarifying distinctions between the old and the young and between individual and group behavior, and in comprehending the underpinnings of participation patterns in adult education activities. We have borrowed directly from such areas as management theory and organizational theory for our concerns relating to the development and operations of agencies and institutions sponsoring adult education programs. We have adopted methods, techniques, and devices from other areas of educational practice that seem useful in the practice of adult education.

Perhaps we have not used the disciplines and professions effectively enough, for we are still haunted by the same fuzziness that prompted us to look for distinctions in the first place. We continue to struggle with the need to justify adult education as a unique area of practice and inquiry. Our task is made difficult by the already acknowledged diversity of the field and by the similarities we share with other areas of professional practice.

This paradox—the presence of diversity amid similarities in practice—calls for less emphasis on distinctions and much greater emphasis on achieving the broadest possible perspective of our field of practice and inquiry. A retreat from a preoccupation with field-level distinctions between adult education and other areas of practice and inquiry in favor of a systems perspective will lead more quickly to the development and refinement of a knowledge base. The remainder of this chapter will offer a justification for such a conviction and will illustrate the application of a new systems perspective to a little-understood characteristic of the field, the organization of adult education. The reader should gain at least the beginnings of a way of thinking about organizations and the processes employed in executing their adult education activities. The framework is intended to suggest a method of analysis that can be applied to the study of adult education and its activities.

Assumptions About Theory Building

A few assumptions about theory building are in order. First of all, it is assumed that the development of theories is a desirable goal for adult education study and practice, if for no other reasons than those at least implied earlier. Second, there appear to be several ways to approach theory development, the particular approach depending on such factors as the subject under investigation, the scholar doing the theorizing, and the stage of development of the discipline or practice. Third, it is desirable not only that the approach to theory development result in theories about the selected subject but also that the process of development lead to an increased understanding of the gestalt of the discipline or practice within which the subject resides. Finally, the road to theory should yield concepts, principles, and propositions that have heuristic value and may be used on an interim basis as they apply to the solution of problems. Theorizing about the organization of adult education will likely produce a variety of approaches that will collectively reveal increasingly more about the nature of the practice, while the material for theory development will be useful to the study of adult education in the near term.

Zetterberg (1965, p. 18), commenting on the nature of theory development in sociology, characterizes two types of specialists in theoretical sociology. The first develops new theories out of his or her own or other people's research; the second draws from a number of "partial" theories to develop a more inclusive theory. A third type may be added—the theorist who draws from a "grand theory" and develops middle-range or partial theories by coupling the former with either his own observations or those of others. There is evidence of all three approaches by researchers and theory builders in adult education, but no single approach stands out as the preferred mode. The development of theory in the field as a whole is at best embryonic and spotty in scope, notwithstanding important attempts at using a "grounded theory" approach (see, for example, Mezirow, Darkenwald, and Knox, 1975); the fruit of single-topic serial research (Boshier, 1976); several related attempts in the area of change, communications, and decision making (Rogers and Shoemaker, 1971; Bennis, Benne, and Chin, 1969); and Knowles' popularization of "andragogy" (the art and science of helping adults to learn) (1970).

A maturation process is implied in a discipline's theory-building efforts. This process begins with the need for definition, and follows with the development of typologies and taxonomies; later, propositions evolve whose systematic interrelationships form the basis of theory. Granted that definitional problems persist even in disciplines that boast highly regarded theories, that new taxonomies and typologies are constantly spawned by new discoveries and ideas, and that theories may rise, fall, or undergo continual modification, a given area of inquiry can nevertheless generally be characterized in terms of its theoretical foundations. Within this context, the study of adult education is more closely identified with the definitional, descriptive stage of growth and development than with the theory and verification stage.

The interpretation of such a simplified overview of theory development and its uses is complicated by the preference of different theorists for different terminology to describe their views. Popular in the adult education literature, for example, are the terms *conceptual framework, models,* and *frame of reference.* In fact, if theory is to have explanatory, predictive, and practical functions, the wiser choice in the present instance may be to stay with the more popular and widely used terms. According to Sztompka (1974, p. 180), "The prerequisite for the construction of a theory is the specification of a *conceptual model* of the domain of reality that is to be explained." He defines a conceptual model as "a set of assumptions defining the fundamental features of that domain." The general assumptions of the model constitute "a frame of reference within which the determinate range of empirical variability is possible." Sztompka further calls for "particular assumptions" of the same model, which signify "concrete decision as to the values of the variables, among those possible on all dimensions of a variability permitted by the general assumptions" (p. 180).

Thus, using Sztompka's terms, the first necessary step in constructing a theory about the organization of adult education would be to specify a conceptual model of its organization. However, the model should not be a mere listing or enumeration of concepts or a vocabulary for speaking about selected phenomena. Instead, such a conceptual model should represent "a complex construct made up of assumptions referring to some selected domain of reality and characterizing it in a simplified or idealized manner" (Sztompka, 1974, p. 31). Hills (1968, pp. 12–13) believes that "description is the fundamental basis of any science" and that "a descriptive frame of reference . . . is a conceptual scheme within which facts about objects are stated. Such schemes consist of a number of concepts . . . which are definitionally related."

To recapitulate, people who would study the organization and processes of adult education need guiding frameworks; so do those who practice the art. Ultimately, we need strong theories to guide our research efforts, but first we need concepts, and clusters of concepts, to frame our thinking and to underpin our practice. Is it possible to pursue the best of both worlds? On the way to theory development through the identification of concepts and construction of conceptual frameworks, we can use the concepts and conceptual frameworks in the more immediate, practical sense.

A Tentative Conceptual Framework

A tentative framework consists of three levels of conceptualization superimposed over empirical referents found in the organized forms of adult education and their processes. The first level is constructed using the concepts and assumptions of general systems theory. The second level utilizes concepts and assumptions of social systems theory, and the third level incorporates specific observation of and experience with organizations and activities in adult education. Figure 1 depicts this relationship.

**Figure 1. A Hierarchy of Concepts
And Assumptions**

General system concepts and assumptions

Social system concepts
and assumptions

Assumptions or
propositions
about
adult
education

Analysis of organizations and processes

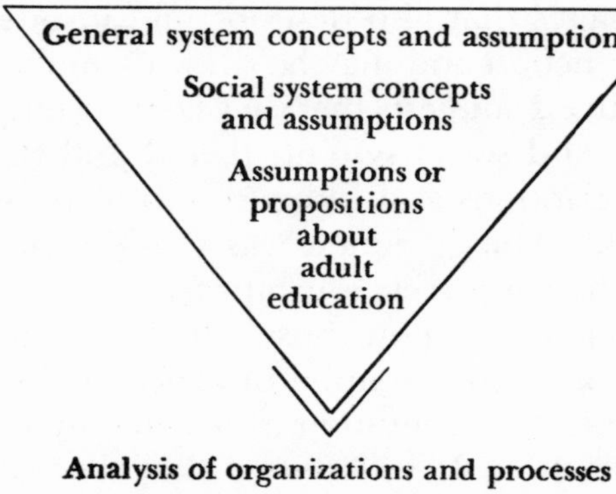

Figure 1 illustrates a hierarchial relationship among the three levels of conceptualization, with all levels framing the analysis of empirical referents. That is, the concepts that describe general systems theory are thought to be more abstract and inclusive than social systems concepts which in turn are broader in scope and more inclusive than propositions about specific organizations and processes in adult education. The relationship between the first two levels of conceptualization is perhaps more easily understood than the relationship between either or both of these and the third level. Whereas social systems are but one type of general systems, assumptions about organized forms of adult education and their processes are not simply derivatives of social systems or general systems. The propositions and assumptions that ultimately form the basis of theory are actually products of the interaction of all levels of conceptualization *plus* empirical observation and verification studies. Figure 2 depicts in another way the relationship that should exist among the various stages of theory development in this area of study.

Figure 2 shows that we need to begin with the development of definitions, typologies, and taxonomies, if for no other reason than to facilitate communication and argument and to provide the descriptive categories within which subsequent inquiry may proceed. Orderly schema are necessary to inspire and help contain descriptive studies. However, in addition to the need for sharp and distinct terminology and categories, there is a need for collections of entities, events, and mental images that also describe and inspire. Concepts perform this function and may be drawn from a wide range of sources. Figure 2 suggests that they be drawn from general systems theory and social systems theory and then be combined with descriptions and categories to form new conceptual frameworks. These frameworks would include relevant concepts and their interrelationships as well as assumptions and propositions built upon those concepts. Finally, theory would result from a combination of conceptual frameworks, their refinement, the generation of testable hypotheses, and empirical verification. It is assumed that the nature of the

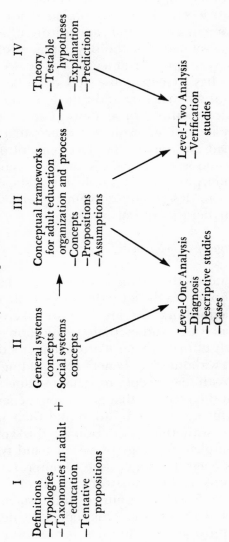

Figure 2. Stages of Theory Development and Levels of Analysis

I

Definitions
—Typologies
—Taxonomies in adult
 education
—Tentative
 propositions

+

II

General systems
 concepts
Social systems
 concepts

III

Conceptual frameworks
 for adult education
 organization and process
—Concepts
—Propositions
—Assumptions

IV

Theory
—Testable
 hypotheses
—Explanation
—Prediction

Level-One Analysis
—Diagnosis
—Descriptive studies
—Cases

Level-Two Analysis
—Verifcation
 studies

resulting theory would be just as fluid as the stages of development that comprise its formulation.

The two levels of analysis provided for by the fore-going development are a significant feature of Figure 2. For example, it is assumed that the development of definitions, concepts and conceptual frameworks is a necessary foun-dation for studies that diagnose and describe problems of organizations (their structure and function) and develop case studies or other methods of analysis. The products of this level of analysis coupled with the conceptual frameworks themselves, lead not only to the development of theory but also to the second level of analysis, made possible by its own theoretical underpinnings. It is only at this stage of develop-ment that we can design and implement verification studies and pursue further theoretical development.

The Present Stage of Development

The state of the art in the study of adult education enterprises emphasizes the left side of Figure 2 more than the right. Adult educators are much more likely to conduct descriptive and case studies than verification studies, and even these early efforts are more often than not designed and implemented without the benefit of guiding conceptual frameworks. With few exceptions, what remains are scattered descriptions and typologies that give a very general profile of organized forms of adult education and their processes. In fact, it is only with the publication of this volume that a reasonably complete typology of systems and types of adult education has been developed (see Chapter Three). There-fore, illustrations of the framework for theory development shown in Figure 2 will be confined to the stage of develop-ment and level of analysis that best depicts the field at present and where it must go next in pursuit of substantive theory. We turn now to a look at the kinds of material needed to form conceptual frameworks. Subsequent sections will dis-cuss the "ingredients" of a conceptual framework, and then case examples will illustrate the utility of the ingredients.

The Potential of General Systems Theory

Two sources of material for the construction of conceptual frameworks will be discussed in this chapter. One is simple observation of existing forms of adult education. By focusing on this source, we will obtain an overview of the state of the art in adult education studies which is consistent with assumptions presented earlier on the value of descriptive studies in the early development of disciplines. The other source of material for conceptual frameworks is general systems theory, which is probably not as obvious a choice of topic for discussion. Some background information and rationale for its value and utility as a major theoretical instrument is therefore presented.

Ludwig von Bertalanffy is credited with first developing general systems theory. Beginning with his classic work in organismic biology, von Bertalanffy spent more than forty years establishing an astoundingly wide-ranging thesis that ran counter to the accepted conceptual paradigm of science, which stressed the reduction of complex phenomena into elementary parts and processes. Von Bertalanffy was convinced that "the fundamental character of the living thing is its organization, and that the customary investigation of the single parts and processes cannot provide a complete explanation of the vital phenomena. Such investigation gives us no information about the coordination of parts and processes" (1975, p. 152). His second conviction was that, in spite of increasing specialization, disciplinary complexity, and the onerous increase in scientific literature, "similar concepts, models and laws have . . . appeared in widely different fields, independently and based upon totally different facts" (1968, p. 33). This parallelism of general cognitive principles in different fields led von Bertalanffy to propose that the existence of models, principles, and laws that apply to generalized systems—regardless of their particular kind or of the relations or forces between them—called for a theory "of universal principles applying to systems in general" (1968, p. 32), hence, the subject matter of general systems theory.

The appearance of structural similarities or *isomor-phisms* in different fields led to the development of the Society for General Systems Research, organized in 1954 under Section L of the American Association for the Advancement of Science. The purposes of the society were (1) to investigate the isomorphy of concepts, laws, and models in various fields and to facilitate useful transfers from one field to another; and (2) to encourage the development of adequate theoretical models in the fields that lack them (Laszlo, 1974). Out of this effort, which characterizes the contemporary aims of general systems theory, is intended to emerge a perspective or paradigm with multidisciplinary applications. Moreover, the movement has spawned countless investigations and publications concerning a variety of interpretations in the areas of mathematical systems theory, systems technology, and systems philosophy. What has finally evolved is a general science of "wholeness" which, until recently, was considered a vague, semimetaphysical concept (see von Bertalanffy, 1968, 1975; Laszlo, 1972, 1974).

How does general systems theory relate to the study of the organization of adult education? First of all, the whole concept of general systems deals with organization—of a living organism, an agency, or a society—and includes fundamental subconcepts that apply to any attempt to understand the dynamics of organization. Second, the relevant concepts can be easily articulated with descriptions and propositions drawn from investigations and observations of the processes of adult education. Third, the scope of general systems theory obviously allows great latitude for conceptual development and theorizing, thus providing a starting point for the development of theories in at least the three modes described in this chapter. Fourth, the concepts, subconcepts, and assumptions of general systems theory are immediately applicable to the analysis of organized forms of adult education and their processes. In sum, we are left with a very general guiding paradigm within which to develop our own conceptual frameworks and to seek the extent of their application to the study of the organization of adult education. The next task is to demonstrate how this attempt proceeds.

A Framework for Development

In order to begin with a methodological framework for examining concepts and assumptions common to general systems theory, we turn to Sztompka's (1974) parameters of conceptual models discussed earlier—models that include both concepts fundamental to general assumptions and more specific concepts fundamental to particular assumptions.

The concept of system appears to be the most fundamental of all concepts. In a very real sense, all other concepts are tied directly to this one, and as will be shown, no other assumptions can be drawn outside of a systems context. A system is defined by von Bertalanffy (1975, p. 159) as "a set of elements standing in interrelation among themselves and with the environment." He further characterized the term *system* as referring to "a model of general nature . . . a conceptual analog of certain rather universal traits of observed entities" (p. 159). This definition includes "real systems, or entities perceived by or inferred from observation and existing independently of the observer . . . and conceptual systems . . . which are symbolic constructs" (p. 165).

The range of concepts related to systems is varied and far reaching. However, the dozen or so concepts that are mentioned most frequently in the systems literature are central to an understanding of the systems concept. These have already been discussed in Chapter One, and the reader is strongly encouraged to refer again to that discussion as a preface for the following. An elaboration of selected concepts follows in order to further our understanding of the nature of general concepts and assumptions thought to be important in the development of a conceptual framework for the study of the organization of adult education.

Two studies have been selected as sources for an elaboration of general systems concepts. To the best of my knowledge, the first is the only study that has addressed the relationship of general systems theory to adult education: Polk (1970) dealt with the application of general systems theory to program planning in adult education, not only developing a suggested model for planning but also thoroughly reviewing the systems literature as it applies to the organization of adult education in general. The second study is a comprehensive and rather ambitious attempt by Laszlo (1974) to develop the framework for a "world order," adopting a futurist's strategy and using general systems concepts for his framework.

Laszlo identified four "basic system invariances," which for him define the unity underlying phenomenal diversity and which, for our purposes, represent a useful synthesis of the fundamental and more general concepts of systems theory. The four "invariances" are: (1) order and irreducibility; (2) self-stabilization; (3) self-organization; and (4) hierarchization.

Order and Irreducibility

All open systems undergo transformations of state; that is, systems are dynamic, growing entities with constant interchanges with their internal and external environments. Amid all of the apparently contradictory tendencies of systems, there is a need for order or predictability in their behavior. The transformations are realized in an orderly fashion, and the system performs its functions with regularity. The concept of order in a system is a means by which a system's structure can be identified. If the structure of a system endures long enough to be identified and recurs often enough to have a name, it is possible to identify some elements of order that are characteristic of it (Laszlo, 1974).

Some systems are more ordered than others, and some system parts may be less ordered than their suprasystem. Although Laszlo claims that more ordered systems are not necessarily "better," it is easier to study and predict their behavior than that of less ordered systems. This is due to the likelihood of the latter to undergo more rapid, frequent, and complex transformations than the former. Order, then, is essential to the stabilization and growth of a system and is of particular concern in the analysis of a system.

The related concept of irreducibility refers to the relationship between the whole system and its parts. In essence, any system is not the simple sum of its parts, and the properties of the whole system are not reducible to the properties of its parts. If order, for example, is seen as a system property, what may be true of the order of the whole system is not necessarily true of the parts of that same system: The parts may be less ordered than the parent system, gaining order only when combining with other parts to make up the whole. Moreover, the interaction of the parts generates properties that were not present in the individual parts. A useful illustration is a social system, in which the characteristics of the whole system are not the same as the characteristics of the individual members of the system. That is, the structure and function of a social system are not representative of the individual human beings whose interactions make up the structure and express the functions of the system. Further, the role of a given member of a social system is not merely the personal expression of an individual but a complex expression of several different members, in interaction, given varying and changing environmental conditions. Thus, the value of irreducibility for the analysis and understanding of systems lies in the distinctions it allows one to make in the analysis of the whole system, its parts (or subsystems), the interaction of the parts, the effects of the interaction on the whole system, and finally the differences that exist in the properties of subsystems and the properties of their suprasystems.

Self-Stabilization and Self-Organization

Self-stabilization and self organization, the second and third concepts discussed by Laszlo, are so closely related that they should be examined together. They relate to the tendency of systems toward a steady-state existence and their pursuit of the dual goals of survival and growth. Survival, however, implies a kind of stability, while growth implies a set of changing internal conditions. These seemingly contradictory requirements actually prompt the system to pursue a state of equilibrium that captures the "best of both worlds" between a static condition of no growth and a condition of chaos. The internal constraints of a system lead it toward stasis, while perturbations from the external environment have the potential of interfering with the system's ability to cope. The steady state, then, is not a static state but one that represents "a level of equilibrium between the internal constraints among the system's components and the forces acting on it from the environment" (Laszlo, 1974, p. 215). To achieve a steady state (the preferred condition), the system must make provisions for self-organization and self-stabilization.

Self-organization helps a system to override homeo-static mechanisms. Self-stabilization returns systems to their preexisting level and state of organization. If we assume that an open system is always vulnerable to its environment and that certain inputs from its environment will stress or stimulate the system in some way, it is clear why a system must develop different levels of potential stability in order to keep adapting to a range of possible destructive environmental fluctuations.

The ways in which systems adapt to their environment are wide-ranging, but in social systems, the best defense seems to be the innovative capacities of their members. As Laszlo (1974, p. 222) puts it, "In sociocultural systems, self-organization occurs by means of innovative change induced by members of a society, either to better cope with internal or external perturbations, or to extend their control capacity over the rest of the social system or its social and natural environment."

Hierarchization

Hierarchization refers to the tendency of all systems to arrange their structures and functions in hierarchies. They seem to do so out of the need to adjust to changing internal and external conditions and to achieve self-organization and self-stabilization. The more systems that become involved in mutual pursuit of common goals, for example, the more likely they are to adopt differentiated functions, specializations, and cooperative networks of relations, and the greater the likelihood of the development of superordinate coordinating systems. Moreover, systems on every level of the hierarchy exhibit the properties of order, irreducibility, self-stabilization, and self-organization (Laszlo, 1974).

A system composed of independently stable subsystems is thought to be inherently more stable and is more likely to withstand extreme fluctuations in its environment than a system built on the same components as its subsystems. Simon (1969, pp. 98–99) has argued convincingly that "complex systems will evolve from simple systems much more rapidly if there are stable intermediate forms than if there are not." Simon offers an explanation by way of the following parable (1977, p. 248):

> Two watchmakers assemble fine watches, each watch containing 10,000 parts. Each watchmaker is interrupted frequently to answer the phone. The first has organized his total assembly operation into a sequence of subassemblies; each subassembly is a stable arrangement of 100 elements, and each watch a stable arrangement of 100 subassemblies. The second watchmaker has developed no such organization. The average interval between phone interruptions is a time long enough to assemble about 150 elements. An interruption causes any set of elements that does not yet form a stable system to fall apart completely. By the time he has answered about eleven phone calls, the first watchmaker will usually have finished assembling a watch. The second watchmaker will almost never succeed in assembling one—he will suffer the fate of Sisyphus: As often as he rolls the rock up the hill, it will roll down again.

Another reason for the rapid growth of hierarchic systems is that a failure in the organization will not destroy the system as a whole, but will only "decompose" it to the next lower stable system level. This enables the development of more complex

structures to start from the next lower level of stability, with
the losses being regained in a relatively short time.

The utility of the concept of hierarchization for the
analysis of systems lies in its potential as a component of a
profiling mechanism. For example, if an actual system is
examined in terms of the degree to which its structure is
hierarchical and the way in which the particular arrangements contribute to the overall functions of the system, it may
be possible to detect weaknesses and strengths of organization and provide directions for changes.

Thus far, the discussion has centered on general system properties. Given the intended emphasis on the organization of adult education, it is appropriate to consider further
sources that are more directly applicable to the specific types
of systems found in adult education. As an intermediate step,
and to be consistent with the frameworks depicted in Figures
1 and 2, a discussion of social systems follows.

A Model of Social Systems

Loomis (1960), a sociologist in search of a framework
for studying change, developed a conceptual model of social
systems to "provide . . . a frame of reference from which to
view empirical data" (p. v). As a rationale for his "processually
articulated structural" (PAS) model, Loomis maintains that
"each science employs a frame of reference or system of
concepts and ideas concerning the pertinent relations of its
special class of phenomena" (1960, p. 1). Beginning with the
premise that the primary concern of social scientists is the
nature of the interaction of people in systems, Loomis set out
to observe the uniformities or regularities of interaction as
they characterized the behavior of social systems. He characterized these uniformities as being orderly and systematic,
with features of reciprocal and interdependent activity. For
Loomis, a social system "implies a functioning entity or
whole, composed of interrelated parts or elements" (Loomis
and Beegle, 1975, p. v). "It is constituted of the interaction of
a plurality of individual actors whose relations to each other

are mutually oriented through the definition and mediation of a pattern of structured and shared symbols and expectations," (Loomis, 1960, p. 4). The social system—clearly a type of general system—has direct reference to the study of the organization of adult education.

The social system model developed by Loomis may be used in an analysis at any level of interaction of people in systems. These applications range from face-to-face interaction of two people to the more indirect, relatively impersonal interaction among members of a society. This method of analysis allows the investigator to move easily from the subsystem level to the suprasystem and back. The important point is that social systems of all types and at all levels possess the same universal elements and processes. An "element" in Loomis' model is "one of the constituent parts of some larger whole . . . [and] is the unit of analysis employed in explaining interaction from the point of view of a given discipline" (1960, p. 5). "The processes articulate each element and all elements in interaction." The processes are also characterized by a "consistent quality of regular and uniform sequences and are distinguishable by virtue of . . . orderliness" (1960, p. 6).

This structural-functional approach to the analysis of social systems is consistent with Sztompka's (1974) approach to theory building, described earlier. Sztompka believes, for example, that "the generalized and relativized concept of system may be specified on two distinct levels of abstraction: the analytic level and the concrete level. On the analytic level the social system is conceived in terms of variables, relations, roles, statuses, etc. On the concrete level, the social system is conceived of people, their interactions, collectivities, groups, classes, etc." (1974, p. 54). Put another way, concepts on the analytic level are abstract, whereas on the concrete level they have immediate empirical referents. This means that Loomis's social systems model is first presented on the analytic level but that it may be used as a framework for studying phenomena on the concrete level. In his most recent work on social systems, Loomis demonstrated an application of an adaptation of his PAS model to change strategies involving educational social systems, governmental social systems, library and mass media systems, religious social systems, and others (Loomis and Beegle, 1975). This particular application of the social system took place in the context of what Loomis and Beegle called a "change agent and change target model," a model familiar to adult educators who use the literature in the area of social change. This model is also closely related to Schroeder's treatment of adult education as "a developmental process used to link various agent and adult client systems together for the purpose of establishing directions and procedures for adult learning programs" (see Chapter Three). Finally, Loomis and Beegle (1975, p. 423) see the PAS model as "an analytical tool . . . needed for analyses of social systems in general." It therefore seems that Loomis's model would be useful in the analysis of a variety of organized forms of adult education.

The following elements of social systems are in Loomis' PAS model:

- *Belief or Knowledge* refers to what members of a system hold to be true, whether or not the beliefs are accepted by others.
- *Sentiment* is closely related to what system members know; it refers to the feelings that members attach to their beliefs.
- *Goals* represent the end, or desired output, of a system.
- *Norms* are the accepted standards, or the "rules of the game."
- *Status role* refers to positions within the system and the expectations applied to the incumbents of the positions.
- *Rank* refers to positions within the system and the expectations applied to the incumbents of the positions.
- *Power* refers to the capacity of system members to influence others.
- *Sanction* refers to the types of rewards or penalties given out by members of a system.
- *Facility* represents the means used to attain system goals.

Related to the structural elements of social systems are *processes*, which "mesh, stabilize, and alter the relations between the elements through time" (Loomis, 1960, p. 6). Social processes are thought to exhibit the qualities of regularity and orderliness, as in the case of osmosis and evolution. Relative to the elements of social systems, there are two types of processes: specialized elemental processes, which articulate how the structural elements are activated and how they relate to certain other elements, and master processes, which articulate several or all of the elements. The elemental processes are ordinarily useful in the analysis of change within systems, whereas the master processes are important in the analysis of total system change.

Briefly, the elemental processes (with related elements in parentheses) are as follows:

- *Cognitive mapping and validation* is the process by which a system's knowledge is developed (belief or knowledge).
- *Tension management and communication of sentiment* are processes that prevent sentiments from obstructing goal-attainment activity or motivate members of a system to achieve system goals and to conform to system norms (sentiments).
- *Goal attaining and concomitant latent activity* is a process by which action is taken to reach the goal of the system's members, including action resulting in both intended and unintended consequences (goals).
- *Evaluation* is the process of assigning values to actions, knowledge, objects, and members of systems, using system norms as criteria (norms).
- *Status-role performance* incorporates both element and process, with role being the process of applying expectations to the incumbent of a position or status (status role).
- *Evaluation of members and allocation of status roles* is a process used to assign status to a member according to such criteria as authority and power, kinship relations, personal attributes, and property holdings (rank).

- *Decision making and its initiation into action* is a process whereby alternate courses of action are reduced so there may be some action within the system (power).
- *Application of sanctions* is a process by which rewards and penalties are distributed to members of the system according to their compliance with goals and norms (sanction).
- *Utilization of facilities* refers to the interpretation of the proper use of system resources in the attainment of system goals (facility).

The master processes are as follows:

- *Communication* is the process by which information and decisions are transmitted among members of systems and is intended to influence beliefs and sentiments through interaction among members.
- *Boundary maintenance* is the process by which the system preserves its identity. Boundaries may be geographic, political, social, or content.
- *Systemic linkage* is the process whereby two or more systems are linked through their sharing of one or more elements in common.
- *Social control* is the process by which deviance from accepted norms is elminated or made compatible with the functions of the system.
- *Socialization* is the process whereby the "heritage" of the system is transmitted.
- *Institutionalization* is the process whereby organizations are given structure and interactions are made predictable.

The above elements and processes may be manifest in both formal and informal ways; hence the frequent references to the "informal power structure" and "formal versus informal communications" in organizations and societies. Moreover, the elements are not always literal descriptors of the intended functions, and the processes are not necessarily absolutes. For example, the element "facility" refers not to the mere presence or absence of certain facilities in a system but rather to the members' perceptions of the proper use of the facilities. Facilities include not only physical or tangible properties but also time, talent, and other intangibles. Therefore, differing perceptions may exist among members regarding proper use of people's time and talents or the use of scarce physical resources of the system. With regard to the absolute versus relative nature of processes, an example would be the relative degree to which members of social systems become institutionalized or identify with the system. In a society, there are varying degrees of identification with established norms, ranging from altruistic suicide (individuals willing to take their own lives because they feel responsible for the system's failure to live up to its norms) to extreme cases of anomie (complete failure to identify with the ways of the system).

For Sztompka (1974), the contribution of each element to the attainment or maintenance of some selected state of the other system elements describes the function of the element. It is therefore safe to say that the elemental and master processes are necessary for the expression of functions of the system elements and are crucial factors in any functional analysis of a system. Finally, Loomis (1960) maintains that, at any given moment, the structure of a given social system may be described and analyzed in terms of the elements of his model. We are left, then, with a model that should serve as an instrument useful in both a structural and functional analysis of social systems.

This brief review of social systems should suffice as an indication of its potential value to the study of the organization of adult education. The serious student would certainly need to pursue the full details of social systems; but for now it is assumed that models such as the above have utility as additional sources of concepts and assumptions for the development of conceptual frameworks in adult education.

Returning to Figure 2, we are reminded that the purpose of this effort is to examine the utility of concepts and assumptions that have potential utility in the development of conceptual frameworks (and ultimately theory) for the study of the organization of adult education. Along the way to theory development, a long-term goal, we hope to demonstrate how the concepts, assumptions, and conceptual frameworks can be used in the study of specific aspects of adult education. Sztompka's distinction between general assumptions and particular assumptions and his call for concepts to be treated on two levels of abstraction (analytic and concrete) now become more useful as they relate to the concepts and assumptions thus far discussed. Sztompka's framework serves as the transition from this point to the application section of the chapter.

Figure 3 depicts the relationship between Sztompka's framework, the ideas expressed in Figure 2, the concepts and assumptions discussed above, and the application stage of development. The figure can be explained by considering the "invariants" of general systems and the components of the social system model as representing general concepts and assumptions, while any directional statements made about them would be what Sztompka refers to as particular assumptions. Examples of the analytic level of abstraction would be the assumptions underlying invariants of general systems and the elements and processes of the social system model; while the concrete expression would lie in the application of the elements to specific empirical referents, such as the analysis of an organization in adult education.

Particular Concepts and Assumptions

In addition to the general, constant characteristics of systems (including social systems), there is a range of variable characteristics of these same systems. The general assumptions of a social system model stress that the elements and subsystems are interrelated but do not specify the types of interrelationships. The types of interrelationships are indicated by the particular assumptions. Sztompka (1974) explains particular concepts as extreme (or polar) types, signifying opposite values along dimensions of variability. Examples of particular concepts and assumptions follow.

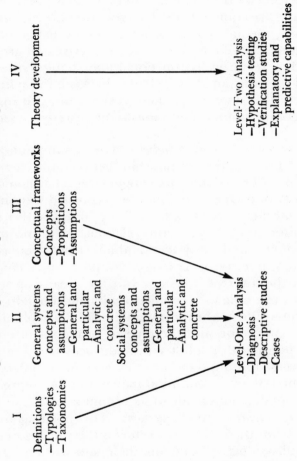

Figure 3. Merger of Sztompka's Framework with Figure 2

I

Definitions
—Typologies
—Taxonomies

II

General systems
concepts and
assumptions
  —General and
    particular
  —Analytic and
    concrete
Social systems
concepts and
assumptions
  —General and
    particular
  —Analytic and
    concrete

III

Conceptual frameworks
—Concepts
—Propositions
—Assumptions

IV

Theory development

Level-One Analysis
—Diagnosis
—Descriptive studies
—Cases

Level-Two Analysis
—Hypothesis testing
—Verification studies
—Explanatory and
  predictive capabilities

Reciprocity versus Exploitation. The specific, polar concepts of reciprocity versus exploitation are related to the general concept of interaction, this last being commonly used in functional analyses of organizations. The assumption underlying reciprocity is that all transfers of values between a system's parts are equitable; exploitation, in contrast, signifies an imbalance, inequity, or disorder in the exchange of system properties. A system is more likely to survive and grow if it is engaged in reciprocally functional interchanges; the less reciprocal the functional interchange between the systems, the less likely the systems or their relationship are to persist, unless compensatory mechanisms are present (Sztompka, 1974).

Consensus versus Conflict. "The assumption of consensus claims that the relationships between the elements (or subsystems) of the system are congenial and harmonious, and the activity of each element may be reconciled with the activities of all others" (Sztompka, 1974, p. 65). Conflict involves antagonistic and inharmonious relationships or incompatibility of elements and subsystems and may result from competition for scarce resources, goal conflict, or incongruities between the aims of a system and the means of achieving them. An example of a conflict-producing situation in adult education would be the incompatibility of the goals of a sponsoring organization and the type of programs offered by a unit responsible for adult education activities. On a more subtle basis, the announced goals and philosophy (beliefs, sentiments) of an organization may not in fact represent the real basis of decisions made by its administrators.

Dependence versus Autonomy. The polar assumptions derived from these concepts refer to the varying degrees to which subsystems depend on their suprasystem. In some cases, the effectiveness of the suprasystem depends directly on the existence of a particular subsystem; in other cases, a subsystem is totally dependent on the suprasystem for its very survival. In some cases the suprasystem continues to exist and pursue its major goals without the presence of certain subsystems. An example is the departure of a highly specialized professional group from a larger professional society, with the aim of forming a separate society of their own.

Isolation versus Structural Context. These concepts refer to the varying dependence and interaction between systems and their environments. In some cases, a system's environment "exerts an important, modifying, and determining influence on the course of intrasystemic events and processes" Sztompka, 1974, p. 69); in other extreme cases, the system is effectively isolated from environmental influences. It is difficult to conceive of the latter case (except in closed systems), although the point of the assumption is that there are certainly varying levels of influence brought about by environmental circumstances. Public institutions of higher education, for example, have until recent years been relatively autonomous in their decision making and in their assuming that the public would continue to provide financial support.

Equipotent versus Differential Functionality. Equipotent functionality means that all elements or subsystems have equal bearing on the behavior of the total system. Differential functionality assumes that, although subsystems are interrelated in a systemic manner, they do not have equal weight in determining the nature of system behavior: some subsystems are simply more important to the survival and growth of a system than others. The system analyst, therefore, has the task of determining the differential effects made by various system components. The purpose of such an analysis would be to determine the relative extent to which each of the components influences overall system behavior.

The preceding paragraphs are only a sketch of a few possible variations of system behavior; but they illustrate the need to specify the range of values that can be attached to the types before any analysis of particular systems begins. The explication of such assumptions about the range of values that can be attached to the types should guide the analyst in any attempt to form judgments about the nature of the particular system's structure and function, given empirical justification. The following brief analysis of one system in adult education will rely on an understanding of these assumptions, as they provide additional meaning to observations of the existing structure and functions of the organization.

The Profile of an Organization: A Systems Perspective

We are now ready to test the "conceptual fit" of the material of this chapter to an analysis of the Adult Education Association of the U.S.A. (AEA-USA). It must be emphasized that we do not yet enjoy the luxury of theories about the organization of adult education, and this example represents something that can be done even while on the road to theory development. The reader should also bear in mind that a thorough analysis of any organization would be beyond the scope of this chapter; therefore, the example is meant to be purely illustrative of what can be done, given more complete development of needed conceptual frameworks.

Our analysis will rest on an "if . . . then" premise. If the organization is to survive and actualize its potentials, then certain conditions of structure and function must be met. The question then raised is whether they are in fact met (Laszlo, 1974). We shall also borrow from Merton (1957, p. 49) in the use of a conceptual framework to diagnose the structure and function of a system:

> First of all, certain functional requirements of the [organization] are established, requirements which must be satisfied if the [organization] is to survive, or to operate with some degree of effectiveness. Second, there is a concrete and detailed description of the arrangements [structures and processes] through which these requirements are typically met in "normal" cases. Third, if some of the typical mechanisms for meeting these requirements are destroyed, the observer is sensitized to the need for detecting compensating mechanisms (if any) which fulfill the necessary function. Fourth, and implicit in all that precedes, there is a detailed account of the structure for which the functional requirements hold, as well as a detailed account of the arrangements through which the function is fulfilled.

This analysis, a normative approach, will profile the AEA-USA against the properties of general systems, broadly conceived, and social systems, in a special sense. The profiling mechanism (or criteria) will represent selected concepts and assumptions from these two areas of inquiry, and the description of the AEA will be taken from my own knowledge of the organization.

AEA's Subsystems

Each of the authors of previous chapters has discussed the Adult Education Association, illustrating the central role that it plays in the lives and activities of adult educators and their enterprises. Indeed, the AEA can be viewed as a microcosm of adult education in American society, representing as it does the variety of institutions, agencies, associations, and individuals engaged in the various forms of adult education.

The association may be characterized as a federation of specialty groups or as a federation of leadership representing the several systems involved in adult education. In this sense, the AEA consists of a variety of relatively autonomous, self-sufficient enterprises that cooperate in pursuit of common goals. The AEA's internal environment includes its affiliates, special interest sections, commissions, councils, standing committees, and executive groups. These subsystems are linked together in a rather loosely defined structure, the functions of which are described in a constitution and manual of procedures.

The diversity of clientele served by the AEA is mirrored in its subsystems. Nineteen special interest sections are organized to appeal to adult educators interested in areas ranging from continuing education in the professions to home and family life education. Five commissions accommodate the unique interests of (1) professors of adult education, (2) adult basic education personnel, (3) women, (4) educators interested in research in adult education, and (5) people concerned with the quality of adult learning environments. These subsystems are formed in much the same way that systems in adult education are born and nurtured—in response to changes in society. For example, the Commission on the Status of Women is said to have developed in response to the "women's movement," an acknowledgement that adult education has a role to play in the further development of that movement.

The potential strength of the AEA is derived from the production and interaction of its subsystems as well as their healthy relationship with their external environment. However, there are signs within AEA that point to a less than optimal relationship among its subsystems. For example, the sections, commissions, and councils interact less with each other than they do with outside systems. Members who associate with particular subsystems relate to members of other subsystems within the AEA not as representatives of their specific groups but as members of the AEA. Their interdependence is defined only by their common membership in the association, not by their common specific interests.

General systems theory assumes that all subsystems tend toward autonomy, or differentiation, from their suprasystem. Examples of this tendency within the AEA are provided by at least two subsystems—the Commission of Professors and the Commission on Adult Basic Education (ABE)—and by the formation in 1953 of another professional association from a section within the AEA. The ABE not only has grown from "special interest" status to become the AEA's largest subsystem but also collects its own membership dues and holds an annual conference of its own in addition to meeting with the AEA. The Commission of Professors has always regarded itself as a somewhat separate entity, at least in terms of its criteria for membership, and often chooses to meet prior to the AEA Annual Conference and in separate quarters. Professors may become members of the commission without joining the AEA, and from time to time, the member professors also speak of secession from the AEA.

As discussed in Chapters Two and Four, the National Association for Public and Continuing Adult Education (NAPCAE) was once a section of the AEA. In fact, the group most interested in the focus of the NAPCAE was once a separate system but merged with the American Association for Adult Education in 1951 to form the AEA. However, a few years later, the group of interested members decided to go it alone once again and form their own autonomous organization. The NAPCAE (then NAPSAE) now has its own subsystems, or affiliates, exhibiting the same tendencies as the larger, more active groups in the AEA.

The growth of subsystems into autonomous systems is often seen as an unfavorable reflection on the parent system. However, the tendency of subsystems to become autonomous should not necessarily be viewed as a threat to a healthy parent organization. A system that provides the input needed by its subsystems is not likely to lose them. Moreover, a secure system with a legitimate place in its own suprasystem (the suprasystem of the AEA is society) will tend to survive through the further development of remaining systems or the addition of other systems or a combination of the two. Every system, however, resists loss of its parts and counters any tendency that threatens its stability. It is only natural that the AEA's loss of a subsystem, perceived as being otherwise consistent with the structure and functions of the parent system, would be seen by most members as a threat to the integrity of their organization. In the case of the AEA, the loss of the Commission of Professors or the Commission on Adult Basic Education would mean not only a substantial reduction in membership but more importantly the departure of powerful voices in the affairs of the association. (Professors have consistently served as leaders in the AEA, and the Commission on ABE is one of only a few subsystems that remain active during the year).

Whenever development occurs in a system, it proceeds from a relatively undifferentiated structure to a state of increasing differentiation and hierarchic order. However, unregulated demands for differentiation lead to disunity and disintegration and ultimately destroy the original system. The tendency of any system is to allow only the degree of differentiation that is absolutely necessary, with its need for stability and equilibrium compelling it to consolidate, regroup, or otherwise hold rein on its subsystems. The AEA's subsystems have grown steadily in number throughout the association's twenty-seven years, reflecting growth in the field and in the ability of the AEA to behave as any other system. It is entirely possible that the present state of the AEA is a typical stage of development experienced by all systems that move from a minimal structure to one of increasing differentiation and is therefore one positive sign of maturation in the AEA. Moreover, the pattern of development experienced by the AEA parallels that of the field of adult education itself.

At least three factors account for the AEA's struggle to contain and integrate its varied subsystems and to maintain its overall organizational health. First, the association has not developed a "hierarchic order" of the sort von Bertalanffy cited as necessary for full development of a system. As noted earlier, the AEA is a loose federation of systems and lacks a structure typical of line and staff organizations. Perhaps it should not become overly "bureaucratized." However, the organizational structure of the Association defies analysis by conventional measures, as evidenced by its failure to exhibit a direct line of authority and responsibility between its executive group and its state and regional affiliates. A second factor affecting its organization is the nature of the inputs provided by AEA to its subsystems. To achieve balance among its parts, a system must establish a reciprocal relationship with them, such that both the subsystems and the parent system receive due recompense for their efforts. For AEA, this means that there is a danger in its relying on two or three of its sections or commissions for internal strength, just as there is inequity and lack of balance inherent in spreading the Associaton's resources so thin that no single subsystem receives enough to prosper and grow. These two seemingly contradictory choices imply that the Association should carefully examine its capacity to serve its sections, commissions and other subsystems that compose its structure. Third, since every system has built into it a homeostatic tendency (or element of self control), there needs to be in every formal organization an administrative structure capable of monitoring and controlling the actions of its subsystems. In AEA, the executive structure is composed of the Executive Committee, the Steering Committee, chairs of the various sections, commissions, committees, and at the policy level, the AEA Delegate Assembly. The general administration of the Association is conducted out of its office in Washington, D.C. by a relatively small staff led by an executive director. The executive group as a whole performs a coordinating or facilitating function and strives to make the association attractive to its members. Beyond that, and in the tradition of a federation-collegial model of organization, authority in the association is granted by some group members to other group members in order to achieve goals of mutual interest. There is relatively little status differential among its members, and all members have the right to participate in the affairs of the association. Moreover, there is neither a screen for recruitment nor a socialization or educational process for new members. This egalitarian approach to organization also allows for voluntary ingress and egress by members of the AEA, and the work of the association depends largely on the voluntary cooperation of its members.

Affiliate Relationships

The AEA's affiliate organizations comprise an important subsystem. However, there is a glaring gap in the AEA's organizational structure between the association's affiliates and the remainder of the organization. Local, state, regional, national, or international organizations with adult education functions may be designated as affiliates of the AEA. Presently, this affiliate relationship is conferred primarily on state and regional adult education associations. An association may achieve an affiliate status with AEA through the payment of one dollar and a declared interest in affiliation. In return, the affiliate may use the AEA's name as a part of its own identification and may become a member of the AEA's Council of Affiliated Organizations, and its president may be a member of the Delegate Assembly.

Not all state and regional associations are affiliated with the AEA, and not all members of affiliates are members of the AEA. This leaves a number of potential member adult educators estimated as high as ten times the current AEA membership.

It appears that people who belong to local associations but not to the AEA do so because of benefits such as lower membership fees, programming that meets local needs, benefits of local lobbying for local legislation, and local contacts. The attractiveness of these benefits to local adult educators and the relatively few benefits of affiliate membership accruing to local adult education organizations may actually comprise disincentives for individuals and local organizations as they consider the merits of a formal relationship with the AEA. At best the result is a low level of mutual interaction and exchange between the AEA and its affiliates.

The Needs of Individual Members

The AEA is largely a membership organization—that is, it caters mainly to the needs of individual adult educators, a fact that is reflected with regularity in its membership drives. The emphasis on the individual naturally assumes that the association's structure and function relate closely to the reasons professional adult educators opt for membership in the AEA. With that assumption, in the late 1970s an AEA Goals and Structure Committee identified what its members thought to be the primary benefits adult educators expect from their AEA membership. These expectations included: (1) resources, including information, technical assistance, funds, and political leverage; (2) professional development, including such factors as improved competencies in their area of specialization, development of leadership talent, and opportunities for advancement through contacts and participation in association activities; (3) a sense of "belonging," reflecting people's universal need for acceptance by the members of whatever groups are most important to them; and (4) recognition or status within the profession and cultivation of an identity as a professional adult educator.

In somewhat different terms, Rice and Bishoprick (1971, p. 75) cite three advantages to be realized by professional group membership: "(1) emotional rewards to the group members from association with others of similar values, ideas, and problems; (2) development of a common technology, enabling a speciality to be taught and thereby facilitating mobility among members of the specialty group; and (3) the evolution of responsibility for a particular role in society, permitting the specialty group to dominate a portion of the social environment."

These advantages obviously overlap with some of the expectations mentioned earlier, such as the need for professional development and methods for satisfying the need. The two lists share in particular the emotional aspects of group membership. There is value in associating with people who are doing the same type of work, speaking the same language, and sharing the same problems. It is reinforcing for a professional to be among peers who share his values or standards of practice (Asch, 1958).

One factor that increases a professional's need to belong is specialization. The more specialized people become in their work, the more interdependent they must become. This dependency prompts individuals to seek support from those for whom their services are intended and from those who share the same special interests. For adult educators, therefore, there is a dual need for group membership: as specialists, they need a market for their product and the support of their specialist peer group; and as adult educators, they share a professional identity that only other adult educators may fully understand.

The AEA's Linkage with the Environment

The association's relevant external systems include all of the organizations with adult education functions mentioned in Chapter Three; other professional associations; potential individual members of the association; funding agencies; international organizations such as the International Council for Adult Education; and coordinating organizations, such as the Coalition of Adult Education Organizations (CAEO). These systems relate to the AEA in a variety of ways: some external systems are linked to AEA subsystems; some outside organizations relate to the AEA as a whole; some relationships are competitive in nature; and in others the AEA is one of several associations whose functions are being coordinated to achieve an overall mission.

In some cases, several linkages exist between a single external organization and the AEA; such is the case with the NAPCAE and the AEA. These two associations share a similar clientele base (although until recent years, the NAPCAE restricted its client system to public school adult educators). The NAPCAE also relates very closely to one of the AEA's most important subsystems, the Commission on Adult Basic Education (ABE). The history of the NAPCAE's relationship to the ABE and the focus of the ABE guarantee overlap in membership and goals of the two associations. The NAPCAE and the AEA also relate to the same coordinating bodies, such as the CAEO, and they have been known to compete for the same funds. They also cooperate in some ways, such as in joint sponsorship of annual conferences. In fact, a dramatic move toward the integration of the two systems was attempted during the 1975 Annual Conference in Salt Lake City, when an effort toward merger of the AEA and the NAPCAE actually resulted in an alternative arrangement involving "union" of various services provided by the two associations.

The 1976 AEA Delegate Assembly reaffirmed and sharpened the intent of the union by adopting a "Resolution on Organizational Renewal." The resolution essentially called for the AEA to take the initiative in establishing "joint secretariat services" with other national associations, to develop a shared publication available to members of cooperating associations, and to set up a mechanism to coordinate regional and local meetings treating interests in common with other associations. It is worth mentioning that the secretariat services were defined as "secretariat services of the organizations entering the union."

The contents of the resolution reflect the influence of a major characteristic of systems—their tendency to maintain their identity and to prevent intrusion of other systems across their boundaries. Systems also tend to be selective in the input they will receive from others and in the output shared with the environment. A principle in systems theory is that the clearer the identity of the system, the tighter the screening devices that help to regulate input and output affecting the system. The nature of this process also reflects the amount of internal control over the system exercised by its executive structure. When boundaries perform adequately, they will permit entrance only of inputs that reinforce a desirable state of existence. Finally, there are identifiable sites in the boundary where inputs are expected to cross, and these entry points are critical to the internal operations of the system. The sites of entry and the control by the executive structure of the kinds of inputs permitted are a measure of the degree to which environmental forces influence the system.

In view of the above boundary-maintenance feature of systems, it is clear why the AEA, as a system with neither a tight organizational structure nor a clear identity, has trouble maintaining its boundaries. When the boundaries are defined in terms of clientele served, location of the system, source of funding, and nature of services rendered to membership, the boundaries themselves are easily confused with the boundaries of other professional associations. Although restricted boundaries do exist—such as regulations concerning who may become members of the AEA Delegate Assembly—boundaries that are shared with other systems are the very ones that are vague and ill defined, related as they are to the total field of adult education. It is also easy to understand why the "union" of the AEA and the NAPCAE is limited to shared facilities and certain identifiable activities (secretariat services, limited publications, and conference activities). It is considerably easier for an organization to change its use of tangible properties than it is to alter its basic value systems and goals. In this case, each assocation is left free to proclaim its right to a territory within the nebulous "suprasystem" of adult education while taking comfort in the fact that it cooperates with other associations. In the absence of major system trauma (such as hopeless financial difficulties and threat of extinction), no system can afford to lose its identity. To do so is to lose its battle for survival.

Conclusions and Implications

The systems approach taken in this chapter is framed at a very general level of abstraction and does not provide all of the details needed for a thorough explanation of the structure and function of the AEA. However, the systems perspective does afford some conclusions about the AEA as a system.

If we examine the AEA in terms of Loomis's model of social systems, it is easy to conclude that certain of the elements and processes are clearly identifiable and functioning while others are not so readily apparent. For example, the broad goal of the organization is to further the growth and development of adult education by accommodating the needs and interests of adult educators and organizations involved in adult education. The goal is certainly broad enough, reflecting the breadth of the AEA's constituencies. The members of the AEA seem to concur with the goal, as evidenced by their willingness to participate in activities designed by the association to reach it. The beliefs and sentiments of its members are less clear, however. They range as wide as the composition of the membership, and reflect a consensus only at the most general level. There is strong belief about the value of educating adults and the value of educational programs specifically tailored to adult needs, but there are varying beliefs about the means of achieving those ends. In fact, there is not even agreement about the ends to be achieved by the various forms of adult education. Hence, the association seeks to serve a variety of constituencies, as expressed by its organizational goal, but those to be served represent a plethora of goals and philosophies of their own.

Concerning the status-role element—the expectations

placed upon positions of leadership within the organization—it seems clear that the federation type of organization militates against a clear delineation of roles and responsibilities within the formal structure of the AEA. This is especially true with respect to the leadership responsibilities of the regional representatives, the various sections and commissions, and the affiliate organizations. For example, the regional representatives have liaison responsibilities between the association and its membership and also relate to the affiliate organizations in their regions. However, the affiliate organizations are represented by a special council within the AEA as well as in the Delegate Assembly. In the latter capacity, they vote through the proxy of members who, with the regional representatives, formulate policy for the association. Another example of ambiguity in status-role relationships is in the tie between the AEA steering committee and the association's executive committee. The former is composed of the elected officers of the association, the executive director, and the fiscal officer. They also are members of the executive committee, which forces them into duplicate decision-making situations each time the two groups meet. In short, the complexity of the federated model lies in the vague relationships of the positions involved as well as the varying expectations held by various parties about the role of incumbents of the positions.

Turning to processes, two observations emerge. First, the systemic linkages between the association and other professional adult education associations are at best tenuous and ill defined. Recalling Griffith's discussion of the problems of coordination (Chapter Four), it is now easier to explain this general lack of coordination among the several associations. Systemic linkage refers to the sharing of one or more elements among two or more systems. In the preceding sections, it was pointed out that the AEA has thus far chosen to share only a minimal number of its elements—namely a portion of its "facilities"—with other associations, probably reflecting mutual sentiment among the associations involved. To share more would soften the boundaries that presently separate the several groups and would invite good reason for not maintaining separate identities. Second, this boundary-maintenance problem is particularly severe for the AEA, inasmuch as it represents such varied clientele and organizations.

These observations exemplify the kinds of conclusions that can be derived from a profile of the AEA as a social system. Furthermore, the conclusions can certainly represent different opinions on the meaning of elements and their functions. The important point at this juncture is that a conceptual framework such as that afforded by the social systems model be used in an organizational analysis of this type.

If we examine the AEA with specific reference to the invariants of general systems (order, irreducibility, self-stabilization, self-organization, and hierarchization), several conclusions are possible. One is that the relationship between the AEA as a total system and its subsystems and its emphasis on individual membership are not particularly conducive to hierarchial development of the association because the AEA has failed to capitalize on the potential strength of the subsystems, building on them to develop an overall structure fully representative of their properties. Moreover, effective coordinating mechanisms are lacking that would provide the AEA with control over the activities of its subsystems. The importance of strong and well-coordinated subsystems is obvious, especially in light of Laszlo's suggestion that a system composed of independently stable subsystems is inherently more orderly and more likely to withstand extreme environmental fluctuations than a system built on the same components as its subsystems. In the present case, the AEA consists of relatively autonomous sections, commissions, and councils, but the association as a whole is composed mainly of the same essential elements as its subsystems—members of the AEA. Assuming the value of hierarchization, the AEA as a system would fare better by building on the carefully cultivated system properties of its own sections and other subsystems, tying them together in a meaningfully interactive and mutually supportive fashion, thereby meeting the needs of members by way of their active participation in the subsystems.

This conclusion also applies to the relationship between the AEA and its affiliate organizations (seen also as subsystems).

Assuming that in a natural system self-organizing and self-stabilizing properties naturally evolve, the AEA as a man-made system shares with other organizations the need for intervening mechanisms that develop these essential properties. There is a concomitant need to encourage innovation among the subsystems and to exploit the talent that members of the systems can bring to the organization. Currently, the AEA is more "reactive" than "proactive" in nature, perhaps again reflecting the nature of the field it represents. However, as discussed earlier, the best defense that a social system has against entropy—and the best offense it can muster for change—lies in the innovativeness of its elements. Growth depends not only on adjustments to changing environmental circumstances but also on a willingness of system members to anticipate and lead in the development of solutions to problems in its internal and external environments. This means that the AEA should not only provide its members with opportunities for elected leadership positions but also systematically cultivate the leadership potential in its ranks. Moreover, the needs of its individual members and its subsystems may very well be met by exploiting the specialized talents within its own ranks.

It seems that the AEA's subsystems exhibit varying levels of dependency on the parent organization as well as varying levels of output. There is relatively little conflict among subsystems; indeed, there is little interaction among them. They function to varying degrees with respect to total system functions; and the members of the subsystems are more likely to be isolated from the functions of the parent system than from external systems. AEA members are characterized more by their primary loyalty to their occupational groupings (for example, adult basic education, business and industry) than to the larger community of adult educators. For this reason, the AEA as a total system is extremely influenced by its environment, simply through the exposure that members and subsystems have to external systems. In this sense, the internal structure of the AEA is potentially subject to a great deal of fluctuation brought on by changing conditions of outside groups. An extreme result of this vulernable state is the loss of important subsystems from the association structure.

The following implications flow from the conclusions that precede. The AEA should strengthen its relationship with its affiliate organizations, with particular attention to establishing a reciprocal exchange of inputs. An incentive for state, regional, and local organizations to affiliate with the AEA should be established (the AEA must also derive benefits from the affiliation). This could be achieved through various means: a new dues structure; an assured line of leadership development extending from the local organization to the apex of AEA administration; the provision of special services by the AEA to local associations; or other ways not yet tried. A strengthened relationship would not only be mutually beneficial to the subsystems and the parent system but would strengthen the system as a whole in the interest of its continued survival and growth.

The sections, commissions, and councils should be the target of continual and systematic development as systems in their own right, so that the AEA can become an association of strong interest groups collectively pursuing mutually supportive goals in behalf of a variety of institutional affiliations and content areas. This subsystem development requires in turn the development of an organizational structure with distinct levels of control and responsibility, ensuring coordination of efforts and development of system components.

Clear lines of responsibilities need to be established among the components of the association, with emphasis on the status and roles of the sections, commissions, councils, and affiliate organizations. A clarification of the association's responsibilities to individual members throughout each of its subsystems is needed. In short, the decision-making functions of the membership should be demonstrably and equitably tied to the several different levels of the hierarchy.

In the pursuit of subsystem development and clear

lines of authority, the association should systematically identify talent within its subsystems that can extend the benefits of the systems themselves. For example, sections may develop the capability of providing technical assistance to their members, thereby helping to meet individual needs for resources.

Provision should be made for the careful cultivation of leadership in the association—beginning with local affiliates and extending through the sections, commissions, and councils—toward the end of developing and ulitizing a wide range of members in leadership positions.

Clear lines of communication need to be established among the subsystems of the AEA to enhance the level of interaction among the growing systems. This recommendation is relevant in the context of any system's need for order in its functions, especially as order in the whole system may compensate for the lack of order in one or more subsystems.

Countless more conclusions and recommendations could be made about the multitude of organizations involved in adult education and the processes through which they accomplish their objectives. The systems framework utilized in this chapter could be used to develop a profile for the field of adult education in general, as was briefly accomplished in Chapter One. In the future, the utility of the concepts and assumptions in this chapter will be studied by the organizations of adult education through the same lens. Eventually we may advance our field of inquiry far enough to formulate substantive theories of the organization of adult education.

Chapter Six

Analyzing the Evolving Structure of Adult Education

K. Owen McCullough

Extracting adult education from its surrounding social milieu—or at least differentiating adult education from the social milieu—is as difficult as determining how many angels can dance on the head of a pin. Is adult education a practice or a program? A methodology or an organization? A "science" or a system? A process or a profession? Is adult education different from continuing education, vocational education, higher education? Does adult education have form and substance, or does it merely permeate the environment like air? Is adult education, therefore, everywhere yet nowhere in particular? Does adult education even exist?

The authors of this volume have not grappled with all these questions; indeed, it was not their purpose to define

adult education. Each of the authors dealt with adult education as if it were a living, healthy, growing entity; as if questions about its existence were moot; as if we only need to
sharpen certain analytical tools—one to describe its many and
varied organizations; another to see how it functions; still
another to look at its apparent lack of coordination and
suggest improvements; and finally one to analyze it as a
system—all toward the end of increasing the knowledge base
about adult education and achieving a certain sense of order.

Each of the authors in this volume has concentrated
on either a structural or operational analysis of adult education (actually a limited structural or operational analysis,
because each has concentrated on a particular structural or
operational unit—the organization or the system—rather
than on the structural or operational whole of adult education). It can be reasonably stated, then, that two things are
evident about adult education: (1) it has organization and
a purpose that can be structurally analyzed and (2) it has a
process that can be operationally analyzed.

In his structural analysis, Knowles dealt with organizations within adult education, but he denied that adult
education is formally organized. In fact, it is not even a loose
federation of organizations, because each of the organizations has its own purposes and activities unrelated (or only
peripherally related) to the other organizations performing
adult education functions. Knowles took a historical look
at adult education, observing that it has grown with no apparent plan, that it denies simplistic description, and that its
vitality exists in its disorder. Adult education does not speak
with one voice; it has a thousand voices, united only with the
philosophical position that lifelong learning is a basic necessity of modern adult existence.

Knowles characterized adult education as a collection
of unorganized organizations, and there is no denying that
much waste and duplication of effort results. But Knowles
does not decry this disorganization; in fact, he celebrates it,
because it frees organizations from external control, making
it possible for them to respond quickly and affirmatively to

adult learning needs. To Knowles, then, adult education is an uncoordinated, unorganized structure that grew out of necessity, responding to the immediate diverse learning needs of adult clienteles. It is a practice, not a program; it is "the art and science of helping human beings learn."

Griffith supported Knowles in stating his case for the coordination of adult education. If an organization of adult education organizations actually existed, coordination of their activities would most likely have been accomplished by now. But whereas Knowles celebrated the strength of disunity, Griffith looked at the weakness of disharmony and noted the benefits to be gained by reducing organizational competition, increasing cooperation and coordination, providing for more efficient use of federal funds, and merging associations. Knowles's conception of adult educators and adult education organizations is reminiscent of a band of wild horses, all going in essentially the same direction but with many strays and much competition for leadership. Griffith would like to establish order within that band—gather in the strays, establish coordination and cooperation among the leaders, develop unifying goals and priorities, and set them all going again, this time in a more steady, orderly fashion. A romanticist might side with Knowles and say, "Leave the horses alone. Watch them defy control and discover their own speed and power." But this is probably not the time for romantic thinking in adult education.

On two points, however, Knowles and Griffith agree: (1) adult education is unorganized, uncoordinated, and leaderless; and (2) it is continuing to subdivide into competing organizations so that it is increasingly difficult for any single voice or organization to be heard above the cacophony of voices and organizations.

Schroeder chose not to deal with the organizational chaos existing in adult education. Instead he analyzed adult education operationally, developing a neat typology of organizations that serve adult education functions directly, marginally, or indirectly. To Schroeder, adult education is "a developmental process used to link various agent and adult client systems together for the purpose of establishing directions and procedures for programs of adult learning." The benefits of this process are provided by a variety of agencies and programs to their respective clienteles. Rather than seeking a locus of control in adult education, Schroeder asked how a practice or process can link various agent and client systems together and be centrally organized, administered, and controlled—especially a process that is universally owned, shaped and sharpened by theoreticians from every discipline, and performed by countless independent practitioners assisting every imaginable clientele. Schroeder defined adult education as a practice or process without central organizational control yet organized within thousands of organizational structures, almost all of them autonomous. Its direction is merely philosophical, provided by hundreds of adult education associations as varied as their members. An adult education practitioner, then, is a process expert, an agent of change, a facilitator.

Peters borrowed general systems theory from sociology and other disciplines and suggested a way to find order and unity in adult education, but without contradicting any of the previous authors. Indeed, Peters would agree with Knowles and Schroeder and might take the same philosophical position as Griffith, calling for more cooperative efforts in adult education. However, Peters revealed how systems theory can be applied to the organization of adult education so that testable hypotheses and confirmed theories eventually can be produced to explain the qualities unique to adult education. The organization of adult education, Peters suggested, is a system having both a suprasystem—the total educational process—and subsystems composed of educative needs, program objectives, and procedures. The concepts and assumptions of systems theory have promise in the development of conceptual frameworks that can be used to study the organization of adult education and ultimately bring it to a new state of coherence. This is a bold proposal, well stated and well argued—and one that contemporary and future scholars may indeed wrestle with—but the immensity of the task may discourage many scholars before even an outline of the task can be sketched.

Where does all this leave adult educators who still cannot perceive an evolving structure in adult education? Indeed, in spite of what a systems theory analysis of adult education produces, is there really organization within adult education? Adult educators function within a distinct process—a system used to achieve educational purposes and provides a basic common goal. But the magnitude of adult educators' diversity combined with that basic common goal has left them in a state of "creative anarchy." It would be incorrect to assume, however, that adult educators have agreed on the futility of developing central organizational structure or an organizational hierarchy in which they could all function in a state of internal order and efficiency. Little if anything has been done even to explore whether organization—formal or informal—actually exists now within adult education. Until now, most adult educators have ignored this task and gone about their business within their individual organizations or associations, either unwilling to grapple with such a task or unaware that it even exists. Moreover, until the recent budgetary problems in countries with unfavorable balances of trade and declining funds for internal improvement, the need for order, efficiency, and reduction of competition for scarce funds was not quite so obvious.

But the world of the 1980s will be budget conscious; the problems of inflation, resource scarcity, and increasing clientele will abound, making cooperation, coordination, and efficiency mutually beneficial for all. The "creative anarchy" of the past and present will become an anachronism: The adult educators who speak for order and organization now command center stage.

The authors of this volume have discovered a plethora of agencies, organizations, associations, agent systems, and client systems with the common thread of process running through them all. The field may seem ripe for organization, but several questions remain: Is organization of a central nature possible? Is it desirable? Is there any virtue left in disunity? Would increased cooperation, coordination, and organization render adult education excessively bureaucratic? Who will lead? Who will follow? Who will decide which funds go where? Who will be served? Who will go unserved? Is it possible to achieve order, organization, cooperation, coordination, and efficiency and still retain the individualistic camaraderie that now exists? Should that individualism be retained?

This volume is destined to be more provocative than instructive, more stimulating than definitive. Like a surgeon's scalpel, it has performed exploratory surgery on adult education. Whether it has exposed benign or malignant parts, is open to interpretation. It has, however, deftly presented complementary analyses of the evolving components of the field.

References

ACKOFF, R. L. "Systems, Organizations, and Interdisciplinary Research." *General Systems,* 1960, *5,* 1.

African Adult Education Association in cooperation with UNESCO. "Seminar on Structures of Adult Education in Developing Countries with Special Reference to Africa." *Final Report.* Nairobi: African Adult Education Association and UNESCO, 1975.

ALDERSON, W., and GREEN, P. E. *Planning and Problem Solving in Marketing.* Homewood, Ill.: Irwin, 1964.

ASCH, S. "Effects of Group Pressures upon the Modification and Distortion of Judgments." In E. E. Maccoby, T. M. Newcomb, and E. L. Hartley (Eds.), *Readings in Social Psychology.* New York: Holt, Rinehart and Winston, 1958, pp. 174–183.

BENNIS, W. G., BENNE, K. D., and CHIN, R. *The Planning of Change.* (2nd ed.) New York: Holt, Rinehart and Winston, 1969.

BLOOM, B. S. (Ed.). *Taxonomy of Educational Objectives: The Classification of Educational Goals. Handbook I: Cognitive Domain.* New York: Longmans, 1964.

BLOOMBERG, W., JR. "Community Organization." In R. M. Kramer and H. Specht (Eds.), *Readings in Community Or-*

ganization Practice. Englewood Cliffs, N.J.: Prentice-Hall, 1969.

BOSHIER, R. "Factor Analysts at Large: A Critical Review of the Motivational Orientation Literature." *Adult Education* 1976, *27*(1), 24–47.

BOULDING, K. E. "General Systems Theory: The Skeleton of Science." *General Systems,* 1956, *1,* 12.

BRYSON, L. *Adult Education.* New York: American Book Company, 1936.

Center for Educational Brokering. *Bulletin of the National Center for Educational Brokering,* March 1976.

The Chronicle of Higher Education. 1978, *16,*(3).

Commission on Non-Traditional Study. *Diversity by Design.* San Francisco: Jossey-Bass, 1973.

Committee of Inquiry Appointed by the Secretary of State for Education and Science. (E. L. Russell, Chairman.) *Adult Education: A Plan for Development.* London: Her Majesty's Stationery Office, 1972.

CROSS, K. P., VALLEY, J. R., and ASSOCIATES. *Planning Non-Traditional Programs: An Analysis of the Issues for Postsecondary Education.* San Francisco: Jossey-Bass, 1974.

DELKER, P. V. "Governmental Roles in Lifelong Learning." *Journal of Research and Development in Education,* 1974, 7(4), 24–33.

DORLAND, J. R. "Role of Professional Organization." In C. Klevins (Ed.), *Materials and Methods in Continuing Education.* New York: Klevins Publications, 1976.

ETZIONI, A. *A Comparative Analysis of Complex Organizations.* New York: Free Press, 1961.

FERRIER, R. *Yours, Mine, and Ours.* Pamphlet describing the Coalition of Adult, Community, and Continuing Education Organizations of Michigan, n.d.

FIELDS, R. R. *The Community College Movement.* New York: McGraw-Hill, 1962.

GAGNE, R., and BRIGGS, L. *Principles of Instructional Design.* New York: Holt, Rinehart and Winston, 1974.

GOULD, S. B., and CROSS, K. P. *Explorations in Non-Traditional Study.* San Francisco: Jossey-Bass, 1972.

GRIFFITH, W. S. "Adult Education Institutions." In R. M.

Smith, G. F. Aker, and J. R. Kidd (Eds.), *Handbook of Adult Education,* New York: Macmillan, 1970.

GRIFFITH, W. S., and CLOUTIER, G. H. *College and University Degree Programs for Preparation of Professional Adult Education, 1970–71.* Washington, D.C.: U.S. Government Printing Office, 1974.

GRIFFITH, W. S., and OTHERS. *Public Policy in Financing Basic Education for Adults.* Chicago: Department of Education, University of Chicago, May 1974.

GRIFFITHS, D. "Administrative Theory and Change in Organizations." In M. B. Miles (Ed.), *Innovation in Education.* New York: Teachers College, Columbia University, 1964.

HARLACHER, E. L. "Community Colleges." In R. M. Smith, G. F. Aker, and J. R. Kidd (Eds.), *Handbook of Adult Education.* New York: Macmillan, 1970.

HEARN, G. *Theory Building in Social Work.* Toronto, Canada: University of Toronto Press, 1958.

HILLS, R. J. *Toward A Science of Organization.* Eugene, Ore.: Center for the Advanced Study of Educational Administration, University of Oregon, 1968.

HIMMELSTRUP, P. *Adult Education in the Nordic Culture: Denmark.* Copenhagen: Secretariat for Nordic Cultural Cooperation, 1976.

HOULE, C. O. *The Inquiring Mind.* Madison: University of Wisconsin Press, 1961.

HOULE, C. O. "The Emergence of Graduate Study in Adult Education." In G. Jensen, A. A. Liveright, and W. Hallenbeck (Eds.), *Adult Education: Outlines of an Emerging Field of University Study.* Washington, D.C.: Adult Education Association of the U.S.A., 1964.

HOULE, C. O. *The Design of Education.* San Francisco: Jossey-Bass, 1972.

HOULE, C. O. *The External Degree.* San Francisco: Jossey-Bass, 1973.

Illinois Task Force on Adult and Continuing Education. *Today and Tomorrow in Illinois Adult Education.* Springfield: Office of the Superindentent of Public Instruction, 1974.

KNOWLES, M. S. *Higher Adult Education in the United States.*

Washington, D.C.: American Council on Higher Education, 1969.

KNOWLES, M. S. *The Modern Practice of Adult Education.* New York: Association Press, 1970.

KNOWLES, M. S. *The Adult Education Movement in the United States.* (Rev. ed.) New York: Holt, Rinehart and Winston, 1977.

KNOX, A. B. *Social Systems Analysis of the Adult Education Agency.* New York: Teachers College, Columbia University, 1967.

LASZLO, E. (Ed.). *The Relevance of General Systems Theory.* New York: George Braziller, 1972.

LASZLO, E. *A Strategy for the Future: The Systems Approach to World Order.* New York: George Braziller, 1974.

LEVY, N. "Learning 1 to 1." *Saver* (a publication of First Federal Savings and Loan Association of Chicago), Summer 1975, 11–13.

LONG, J. S. "Alberta's Local Further Education Councils." *Adult Leadership*, 1976, *25*(3), 83–88.

LOOMIS, C. P. *Social Systems: Essays on Their Persistence and Change.* New York: D. Van Nostrand, 1960.

LOOMIS, C. P., and BEEGLE, J. A. *A Strategy for Rural Change.* New York: Halsted Press, 1975.

LUMBERG, G. A., SCHRAG, C. C., and LARSEN, O. N. *Sociology.* New York: Harper & Row, 1963.

MACCOBY, M. *The Gamesman.* New York: Simon & Schuster, 1976.

MCGREGOR, D. M. *The Human Side of Enterprise.* New York: McGraw-Hill, 1960.

MAGER, R. S. *Preparing Instructional Objectives.* (2nd ed.) Belmont, Calif.: Fearon, 1975.

MASLOW, A. H. "A Theory of Human Motivation." *Psychological Review*, 1943, *50*, 370–396.

MERTON, R. K. *Social Theory and Social Structure.* New York: Free Press, 1957.

MEZIROW, J., DARKENWALD, G., and KNOX, A. *Last Gamble on Education.* Washington, D.C.: Adult Education Association of the U.S.A., 1975.

National Advisory Council on Adult Education. *Interim Re-*

port. Washington, D.C.: National Advisory Council on Adult Education, 1971.

National Advisory Council on Adult Education. *An Historical Perspective: The Adult Education Act, 1964–1974.* Washington, D.C.: National Advisory Council On Adult Education, 1974.

National Advisory Council on Adult Education. *1976 Annual Report.* Washington, D.C.: National Advisory Council on Adult Education, 1976.

National Advisory Council on Extension and Continuing Education. *A Question of Stewardship: A Study of the Federal Role in Higher Continuing Education.* Washington, D.C.: National Advisory Council on Extension and Continuing Education, 1972.

National Center for Education Statistics. *The Condition of Education, 1975.* Washington, D.C.: U.S. Government Printing Office, 1975.

"New Imperatives Drafted at Wingspread." *Adult and Continuing Education Today,* 1976, *23* and *24,* 1–2.

North Carolina State University. *Master Bibliography.* Raleigh: Department of Adult and Community College Education, North Carolina State University, 1974.

OPTNER, S. L. *System Analysis for Business and Industrial Problem Solving.* Englewood Cliffs, N.J.: Prentice-Hall, 1965.

Organization for Economic Cooperation and Development. "Learning Opportunities for Adults: Framework for Comprehensive Policies for Adult Education." (1st Revision.) Paris: Organization for Economic Cooperation and Development, November 1975 (mimeographed).

Organization for Economic Cooperation and Development. "Comprehensive Policies for Adult Education." Paris: Organization for Economic Cooperation and Development, 1976 (mimeographed).

PETERS, J. M. and BOSHIER, R. "Adult Needs, Interests, and Motives." In C. Klevins (Ed.), *Materials and Methods in Continuing Education.* Los Angeles: Klevins Publications, 1976.

PETERSON, R. E. *Postsecondary Alternatives to Meet the Educational Needs of California's Adults.* Final Report of a Feasibility Study

Prepared for the California Legislature. (No. 432.) Sacramento: Assembly Publications Office, September 1975.

POLK, C. H. "An Application of General Systems Theory to Program Planning." Unpublished Ed.D. Dissertation, North Carolina State University, 1970.

Postsecondary Education Resources, Inc. *The PER Report*, August 2, 1976, *1*, 2, 5.

Resource Group on Continuing Education and Community Services. *In Support of Lifelong Learning*. Hartford: Connecticut Commission for Higher Education, July 1975.

RICE, G. H., and BISHOPRICK, D. W. *Conceptual Models of Organization*. Englewood Cliffs, N.J.: Prentice-Hall, 1971.

ROGERS, E., and SHOEMAKER, F. *Communication of Innovations*. New York: Free Press, 1971.

SCHROEDER, W. L. "Adult Education Defined and Described." In R. M. Smith, G. F. Aker, and J. R. Kidd (Eds.), *Handbook of Adult Education*. New York: Macmillan, 1970.

SCHROEDER, W. L. "Adult Education in the United States." In *Adult Education in Five Continents*. Stuttgart: Kohlhammer Company, 1977.

Scottish Institute of Adult Education. "Adult Education: The Challenge of Change." *The Alexander Report: A Summary*. Edinburgh: Scottish Institute of Adult Education, 1975.

SIMON, H. A. *The Sciences of the Artificial*. Cambridge, Mass.: M.I.T. Press, 1969.

SIMON, H. A. *Models of Discovery*. Boston: D. Reidel, 1977.

SMITH, R. M., AKER, G. F., and KIDD, J. R. (Eds.). *Handbook of Adult Education*. New York: Macmillan, 1970.

Studies in Social Significance of Adult Education. New York: Macmillan, 1928–1932.

SZTOMPKA, P. *System and Function: Toward a Theory of Society*. New York: Academic Press, 1974.

THEODORSON, G. A., and THEODORSON, A. G. *A Modern Dictionary of Sociology: The Concepts and Terminology of Sociology and Related Disciplines*. New York: Crowell, 1969.

UNESCO. *National Coordinating Bodies of Adult Education*. An Interim Report. Paris: UNESCO, 1974.

UNESCO. "Draft Recommendation on the Development of

Adult Education." 19c/24. Paris: UNESCO, August 16, 1976 (mimeographed).

U.S. Civil Service Commision. *Employee Training in the Federal Service.* Washington, D.C.: U.S. Government Printing Office, 1976.

U.S. Congress. *The Education Amendments of 1976.* 94th Cong., 2d sess., Conference Report. Title I, Part B, P.L. 94-482.

U.S. National Advisory Council on Extension and Continuing Education. *A Decade of Community Service and Continuing Education: Tenth Annual Report.* Washington, D.C.: U.S. National Advisory Council on Extension and Continuing Education, 1976.

VERNER, C. "The Structure of Community Adult Education." In W. C. Hallenbeck and others (Eds.), *Adult Education Theory and Method.* Chicago: Adult Education Association of the U.S.A., 1962.

VERNER, C. "Definition of Terms." In G. Jensen, A. A. Liveright, and W. Hallenbeck (Eds.), *Adult Education: Outlines of An Emerging Field of University Study.* Washington, D.C.: Adult Education Association of the U.S.A., 1964.

VERNER, C., and BOOTH, A. *Adult Education.* Washington, D.C.: Center for Applied Research in Education, 1964.

VON BERTALANFFY, L. *General Systems Theory.* New York: George Braziller, 1968.

VON BERTALANFFY, L. *Perspectives on General Systems Theory.* New York: George Braziller, 1975.

WEINER, S. B. "The Politics of Transition: Adult Education in California." *Phi Delta Kappan,* 1977, *58*(5), 412–414, 417.

World Confederation of Organizations of the Teaching Profession. *Proceedings of the Ninth WCOTP Invitational Seminar on Adult Education.* Morges, Switzerland: World Confederation of Organizations of the Teaching Profession, 1975.

ZETTERBERG, H. *On Theory and Verification in Sociology.* Totowa, N.J.: Bedminster Press, 1965.

Index

171